Acknowledgements

An online reader not long ago wrote to me and said simply, "You're a rich man, John McWade." By which he was referring to the trust that so many of you have placed in me, and the fact that I can pose, in his case, a simple question, and so many are willing to pitch in and help.

In this way, I am indeed rich. *Before & After* has the world's best audience—curious, creative, expressive, loyal. Some of you have been with us for 20 years. Some we hear from often, others rarely. Some of you are a visible part of our lives, contributing directly and obviously to our work. With others, we gladly share our hours and our confidence. Still others team with us and work to a common vision.

This book is the product of such teamwork.

I'd like to thank our friend Michael Solomon, without whom we could not have gotten our second start. Thank you to our industry colleagues, whose co-operation—in the full sense of the word—has yielded new markets, new revenue, and, not least, moral support. And thanks to Seth Godin and Sean D'Souza, friends and foils who see the world differently than we do and provide valuable perspective.

Closer to home, there's my staff. My wife Gaye, without whom I would be someone else, someone smaller. Dexter Abellera, our talented and tireless senior designer, whose work fills the pages of this book; e-mail Dexter at 3:00 a.m. and you'll probably get a reply. And our unnamed Webmaster, not shy but secretive anyway, who keeps us online and, basically, in business, with her abundant technical skills and her care. Her name is Dr. Evil.

I'm delighted to thank the hardworking crew at Peachpit Press, who pretty much hounded us into making this book. (This is a good problem to have!) I'll start with publisher Nancy Ruenzel and add editor Cathy Lane, who also edits LogoLounge.com. Both, once upon a time, were competitors of ours but then came over from the Dark Side. Nikki McDonald is the acquisitions editor who got this project launched and has kept it sailing smoothly. And thanks to Kim Scott, who has now laid out all three of our books, and production manager Tracey Croom.

None of us ever creates anything alone, and I am grateful for every one of you who, in ways large and small, visible and invisible, has helped shape *Before & After* into what it is today.

Contents

Before&After.
HOW TO DESIGN COOL STUFF

By John McWade

Before & After: How to Design Cool Stuff
John McWade

Peachpit
1249 Eighth Street
Berkeley, CA 94710
510/524-2178
510/524-2221 (fax)

Find us on the Web at: www.peachpit.com
To report errors, please send a note to errata@peachpit.com

Peachpit is a division of Pearson Education

Copyright © 2010 by JMS Publishing

Project Editor: Nikki Echler McDonald
Production Editor: Tracey Croom
Development and Copy Editor: Cathy Fishel Lane
Indexer: Ken DellaPenta
Cover design: John McWade
Interior designer and compositor: Kim Scott, Bumpy Design

ISBN 13: 978-0-321-58012-2
ISBN 10:   0-321-58012-5

9 8 7 6 5 4 3 2

Printed and bound in the United States of America

Projects

Introduction

This book, like the two before it, is a compilation of articles that first appeared in our magazine, *Before & After, How to design cool stuff.*

Before & After, for you who don't know, is a magazine that teaches graphic design. A better way to say it would be that it's a magazine that explains graphic design, or illustrates it, because we don't teach in the sense of conducting a formal course of study, where skills are learned in a sequence, each building upon the last.

What we do is show it, typically with a real-life project, and explain what's going on—why *these* colors go together (or not), why *this* object must be bigger than *that* object to convey thus-and-such a meaning, and so on.

Some people get this kind of instruction in school, but most do not. Most of us are like you. You know some about design, you have an interest in it, and you have a need for it.

Maybe you have a brochure to write.

Or a slide presentation to make.

Or a newsletter to edit.

Or a Web site to build.

Maybe you need a logo for your new business. Or an ad. Or a DVD cover.

Whatever the case, you have a story to tell that has some kind of visual expression, meaning that it can be *seen.* That's where design comes in.

Inherent in the meaning of design is the idea of planning. To design a building or a garment or even a business means to plan it, then actually work the plan.

Graphic design, of course, means to plan the visual presentation of a thing. Design is about *how it looks,* but there's more, because how it looks can't be separated from what it says and does.

There is a process to design, and the key step is the first one: Decide what needs to be achieved. Ask, in other words, *where are we going?* Once you know, you work out what needs to be said, the concept you'll use to say it, the elements—type, colors, images, and so on—that will express the concept, then you work them together into the finished piece.

Before & After does this in the real world.

We've arranged this book in three sections: Knowledge, Technique, and Projects. Because every design has all three, they naturally overlap.

Knowledge is about the basics. Basics are called *basic* not because they're simple-headed but because they are the basis, or foundation, of every design. Basics include line, shape, direction, motion, scale, proportion, similarity, proximity, color, composition, and so on. You learn the basics because they make your work easier and your designs better.

Technique illustrates practical ways and methods. What's valuable about this section is its transferability. The way you crop photos on this brochure can be repeated on that Web

page. The way you set your type or handle a margin or overlap an object in this advertisement can be done again in that newsletter. Some techniques have a big effect and make dramatic designs and because of that are obvious. Others are influential but small and can be repeated forever unnoticed. All have their place. You'll see.

Projects are whole jobs—brochures, newsletters, Web sites, business cards, slide presentations, and logotypes—in which knowledge and technique come together and work. Projects show concept and application at once—what's been done, how, and especially *why*. Our projects also make great blueprints for your projects. You can, more or less, copy our designs, and use our knowledge to make them work for you.

Twenty years ago when we were dreaming up this adventure called *Before & After*,

I recall one day driving around thinking how to describe what the magazine would be about. "Graphic design for desktop publishers" was as close as I'd gotten. It would show how to design newsletters (big at the time), brochures, stationery, and other business documents. It would illustrate design concepts and how to set type. It wasn't about point-and-click but rather about the aesthetics—the whys and hows of good visual communication.

But it was too much. There are too many different aspects of design to summarize in a sound bite. "How to do page layout" not only didn't describe it fully, it was dull, too. And *Before & After* wasn't about *dull*: It was about *cool. Cool stuff.*

So why not just call it that? I asked out loud in the empty car. *How to design cool stuff.*

And that's what it became. I hope you find this book enables you to do exactly that.

—John McWade

Knowledge

Design without rulers

Put away your ruler. Here's how to design the way you see.

Ever watch a street artist at work? What fun! A splash here, a dash there, and from a blank canvas a picture just… *appears*. He uses no mechanical tools at all, no columns, rulers, or guides, yet the result is a beautiful whole. *It's so fluid.*

The best design is like that.

To see how it works, let's design a page, but instead of a grid, we'll use this picture—*what we see*—as our visual guide. Its lines, shapes, proportions, and their relationships will govern our choice of type, sizes, colors, layout, and everything else.

What can you see?
Measuring only by eye (closely, not exactly), can you answer the following?
- Is the man as tall as the globe?
- Is the man as wide as the pot?
- How many pots wide is the tree?
- What else in the picture is the size of the pot?

1 Take a visual inventory

Every image has lines, shapes, textures, colors and so on that can guide a design. First step is to take a visual "inventory." Start with the big elements.

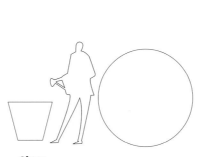

Basic shapes
The image is made of three basic shapes.

Sizes
It has a hierarchy of small, medium, and large elements.

Layout
The composition is fairly balanced.

Focal point

A good image has a focal point. This image has two—one physical and one phantom.

Physical
The primary focal point is usually the biggest, clearest, or most vivid object in the image—in this case, the globe.

Phantom
The three forms create a compositional triangle, the center of which—just what you'd want— is on the money. The center is the strongest point of any visual field.

Secondary
The phantom is reinforced by the focal center of the white triangle. Had you noticed it?

Objects and spaces

The objects and spaces in this image are unusually repetitive.

The pot is the same size as the space above it...

...and the size of the space beside it.

It's the same size as North America!

Close enough...

Artistic relationships are perceptual, not mechanical. If it looks close enough, it really *is* close enough, so inventory only by eye.

The image is four pots tall.

A one-pot space encircles the globe.

The man fits a pot space.

A natural grid

This image has a natural grid that is unusually uniform. Its elements are so repetitive that they create a whole grid!

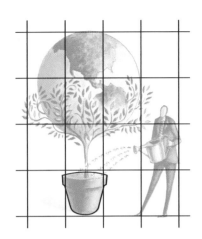

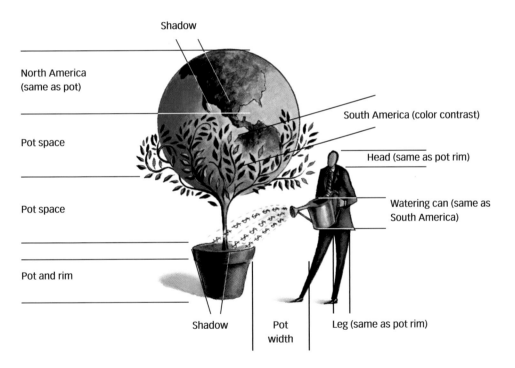

Shadow

North America (same as pot)

Pot space

Pot space

Pot and rim

Shadow

Pot width

South America (color contrast)

Head (same as pot rim)

Watering can (same as South America)

Leg (same as pot rim)

Smaller elements
While you're looking at the large elements, make note of the smaller elements, too. Pay attention to edges and contrasts. Clear edges are like the man's head and legs. South America stands out because of its color contrast. The shadow areas have obvious weight, and so on. Take the time to consciously observe these things. What you're doing is training your eye. It will soon become intuitive.

Shape and texture

Be aware of what the lines are doing. Note if they're straight or curvy, where they're close or far apart, where they change direction, and so on.

Far (phantom lines)

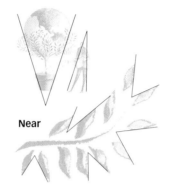

Near

Look at all the triangles! These create visual movement.

Triangles are evident at every distance from farthest to nearest.

The edges create a repetitive texture; note the pointiness throughout.

2 Choose colors

The next step is to create a color palette from the image.

A bazillion pixels!
Color plays a major role in design. The easiest and best place to get a perfectly coordinated palette is the image itself. First, reduce its thousands of pixel-size colors (right, inset) to a workable few by applying Photoshop's or Illustrator's built-in *Mosaic* filter (far right). Rarely will you want more than 64 colors, and usually 32 or even 16 are better. For fewer colors, increase the Cell size; for more, decrease it.

Organize

Sample color swatches with the eyedropper tool, then arrange all of the swatches by color and value.

You can see in *Mosaic* mode that the image has several major colors—the blues and greens of the globe, terracottas of the pot, and grays of the man. Sample dark, medium, and light pixels from each (below left). Neatly arrange your choices by color, then by value (dark to light). Take the time to actually do this; you'll be surprised by how much it helps you visualize. Sample a few minor colors—in this case, yellows and violets—that can be used for complements and counterpoints. Discard lookalikes.

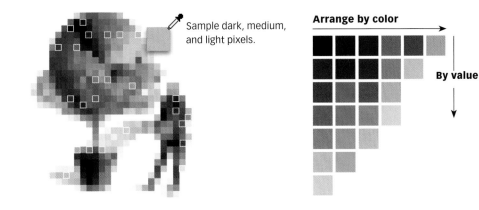

Sample dark, medium, and light pixels.

Arrange by color

By value

Try each one on

Try the image atop a swatch of each color. What you'll see is that every color you picked automatically coordinates, because it's already in there!

Cool colors
Cool colors are more direct and somewhat businesslike and aloof. The blue globe now blends into the background, and those opposite oranges stand out.

Warm colors
Warm colors are soft, earthy, welcoming, suitable for environmental messages. Note how the blue globe stands out against its opposite colors, the terracottas.

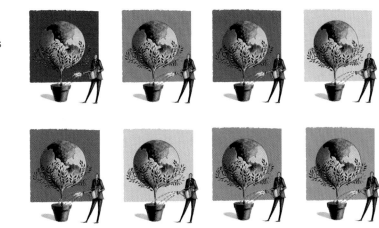

Next, we need to select a typeface that feels like the image.

There are many ways to choose a typeface. You may have a house style, so no choice is required. You may have a look already in mind—say, formal or businesslike or collegiate. You may have a new favorite to try out, which is always fun. Whatever the case, keep in mind that type is graphical, just like an image. Its lines will sweep or jog or dive. It will have tooth and grain. When you add type to a design, its visual characteristics interact with those already on the page, for better or for worse.

For this article, the image is driving our choices. Our goal is to match the visual properties of image and type. Our type choice must also be functional—beautiful, readable, and reproducible.

So what's here? We've seen that the image is full of texture: It has a rich, detailed surface and a lot of "leafy-ness." The leaves are pointy, evenly spaced, and they actually look a lot like serif type.

Let's take a look at typefaces in three common categories to discover what similarities we can find.

Glypha   slab serif

Myriad Pro   sans serif

Galliard   serif

Three viewing distances

Compare the type to the texture at three distances—near, middle, and far; it will look different at each. Many typefaces are better at one distance than another.

Glypha is outdoorsy

A beautiful slab serif with perfect letterfit, Glypha is boxy and clean, with hard edges and repetitive shapes. It's excellent in both headlines and text—an uncommon asset—and its bold, slab sides make it a natural for outdoorsy nature of the art. Glypha is also very easy to read. Problem? It looks nothing like the image.

Near

Middle

There has never been a greater opportunity for private enterprise to do good for everyone on earth by creating new business growth in the green sector. Join us today as we explore how to deploy capital resources in industry, technology, research and communications, locally and across international boundaries, for both private and public benefit. To reserve a seat, log onto www.greenenergysummit.org.

Far

There has never been a greater opportunity for private enterprise to do good for everyone on earth by creating new business growth in the green sector. Join us today as we explore how to deploy capital resources in industry, technology, research and communications, locally and across inter-

Turn it upside down

A reliable way to "see" a typeface is to turn it upside down, which reveals its ridges, hollows and, funny knicknacks that are always felt but normally unnoticed.

Myriad Pro

Myriad is crystal clear

For outright visual clarity, there is probably no typeface better than Myriad. Extremely good in headlines and short passages of text, Myriad's large, open counters and minimal forms retain their clarity at even the lowest resolutions. Myriad projects a light, fresh, clean look that's a natural for green topics, but it doesn't look like our image.

Near

Middle

There has never been a greater opportunity for private enterprise to do good for everyone on earth by creating new business growth in the green sector. Join us as we explore how to deploy capital resources in industry, technology, research and communications locally and across international boundaries for both private and public benefit. To reserve a seat, log onto www.greenenergy.com

Far

There has never been a greater opportunity for private enterprise to do good for everyone on earth by creating new business growth in the green sector. Join us for a day as we explore how to deploy capital resources in industry, technology, research and communications locally and across

Watch the surface

While you're comparing lines and edges, pay attention to surface texture, too. Note the leaves are irregular and grainy, with a mottled blend of colors.

Galliard

Galliard Roman is textured
Galliard is a Roman typeface with chiseled features and sharp, exaggerated serifs. Its thick-to-thin strokes help make Galliard easy to read, although its angles would be tiresome in large amounts. It comes in several weights, it's well proportioned, it has the easy familiarity of serif type, and *it looks like the leaves!* Galliard will be our choice.

Near

Middle

There has never been a greater opportunity for private enterprise to do good for everyone on earth by creating new business growth in the green sector. Join us for a day as we explore how to deploy capital resources in industry, technology, research and communications locally and across international boundaries for both private and public benefit. To reserve a seat, log onto www.greener-

Far

There has never been a greater opportunity for private enterprise to do good for everyone on earth by creating new business growth in the green sector. Join us for a day as we explore how to deploy capital resources in industry, technology, research and communications in

4 Layout

Layout is where those lines, shapes, spaces, colors, and textures finally get put to work. We'll illustrate how by designing a legal-size brochure page.

Work to the image

First step is to place the image on the page. Where, and how big? The key is to have visible relationships. Because the globe and its pot have a strong central line (right), center page will be its strongest position, where each will reinforce the other. (Remember, it's center-*ish;* none of this is ruler exact.) Similarly, the pot space we saw encircle the globe will be visible as a top margin (right).

For this design, we've hidden the non-printing fold lines (left); we care only about what the eye can see.

Legal-sized brochure, 14" x 8½"

Set the headline

A rule of design is to work with what's in front of you; don't arbitrarily make stuff up. Here, the headline picks up the visual characteristics of the globe.

Type based on size, color, and texture

(Right) Placing a headline across the top is normal, but don't do it; the straight, horizontal line is a *foreign object* that's different from what's in front of us. Instead, a block of overlapping lines in Galliard Ultra mimics the size, mass, color, and texture of the globe, a visible relationship. Its position beside the globe (below) strengthens the connection. Note how the interaction of translucent serifs (white inset, below, right) mimics the size and texture of the leaves. Margins are unaligned in any way.

Add photos and text

As you add things to the page, its complexity increases, and it becomes increasingly difficult to sustain visual coherency. Pay attention to what's happening *around* your material—in the margins, at the edges, between things.

Rectangular space, organic design

A paradox of design is that while nature is organic and irregular, paper and text blocks are rectangular. These rectangles have strong and often unwanted visual presence, and it's a challenge to "unrectangle" a page without messing up the reading. But there are ways. In this case, the photos and text remain unaligned, yet meander downward following the general contours of the globe (left). Unlike a standard text wrap, make sure that no identifiable white shapes form between elements.

Toothy texture

(Left) Set in Galliard Ultra and colored like the globe, the speakers' names stand out from the surrounding text, while the whole paragraph has the texture of the illustration, an easy blend of form and function.

Align to the paper

The paper is also an active element that can be used as needed. Here, the lead paragraph and key details are aligned right to an edge, establishing a visual anchor.

Parallel lines have an automatic relationship.

That recurring pot space

If you've taken the time to thoroughly inventory your image, you'll find yourself seeing (or feeling) things you'd otherwise miss. Above, the pot space recurs almost intuitively between elements on the page. As a result, while the layout appears only loosely structured, it has real coherency that's felt more than consciously observed. Note also that the lead text block in the upper right, like the headline across from it, is the general size and shape of the globe, another intuitive setting.

Descending sizes

Finally, text aligned right descends to the lower-right corner, the natural exit point of the page, in increasing detail. Note that the ragged-left edges meander loosely around the image as before.

The empty page has a lot to say

Don't fly past that setup dialog! It's where your design begins!

A blank page may have nothing on it, but it's the most important *nothing* a designer will encounter. It is the platform upon which great design is built. It is here that you establish your world—the dimensions of your page, its orientation, its active space, and whether it appears alone or in pairs. These choices affect how the page is perceived, how it's touched, how it's read, and ultimately, its success.

Which page size does what? Where does a reader's eye go? What does empty space do? Here are some answers to questions you didn't know needed asking.

Page size →

Margins →

→ Orientation

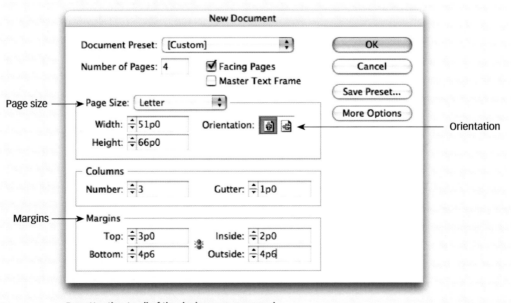

Pay attention to all of the design resources and options available to you before you click OK.

Why are movies at the theater better than movies at home? Because they're so BIG! They thunder, they fly; our heads must turn to follow the action. At home we can see the whole scene at once. The difference in size is one not of performance but of perception, and it plays a vital role in our experience.

We relate image size to our own size. It is our human scale that governs how we see.

In print, our focal "zone" is a space roughly the size of our own head—at reading distance, about a letter-size sheet. A design in this space will be perceived as a whole. A tabloid, at twice the size, is too big for a single view; to take it in our eyes must move, so we see it (and it must be designed) in sections.

Our perception of a page is also influenced by its proportions. We think differently of a tall, narrow page (airy) than a square one (earthy). The ideal proportion has for millennia been considered the "golden rectangle," a ratio Renaissance mathematicians defined as 1 to 1.618. The Greek Parthenon is a golden rectangle. Golden proportions can be found in windows, tabletops, photos (3″ x 5″, 4″ x 6″, etc.) and the human bust. Generally speaking, the most pleasing rectangle has a length one and a half times its width.

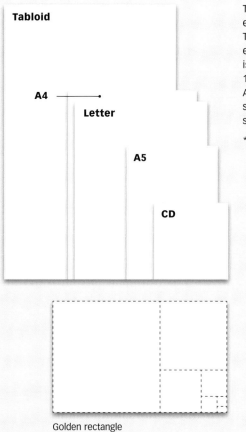

To run on modern presses, aesthetics must often yield to efficiency, which means employing standard paper sizes (left). The International Standard A Series (below) illustrates how efficiently small sheets are made from large ones. The A series is based on a size called the A0, a rectangular sheet 841mm by 1189mm* (33⅛″ by 46¾″). Cutting an A0 in half produces two A1 sheets, cutting an A1 in half produces two A2 sheets, and so on. Every sheet in the series, no matter how small, has the same shape.

*One square meter in area

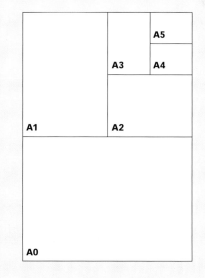

Golden rectangle

A page can be folded crosswise or lengthwise, in halves, thirds, quarters, or asymmetrically. A folded document has heft and substance that a flat sheet does not. And while a flat page reveals its contents all at once, a folded document hides some to be revealed later, a tantalizing opportunity for the designer.

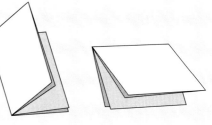

Fold in half in either direction...

...or twice to make a note card that prints on a single side.

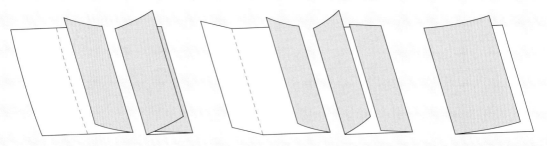

Letter fold

Gatefold

Off-center fold

2 │ Orientation

Orientation refers to how the page is placed in front of us. A tall page "looks in"—that is, the reader focuses on its visual center. A wide page "looks out," meaning the reader looks to the right and left margins, wanting to see the entire sheet at once.

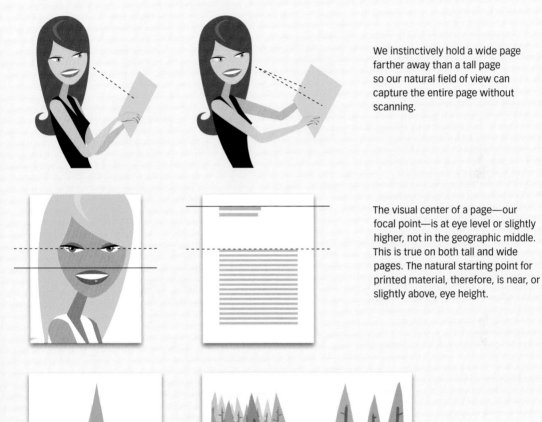

We instinctively hold a wide page farther away than a tall page so our natural field of view can capture the entire page without scanning.

The visual center of a page—our focal point—is at eye level or slightly higher, not in the geographic middle. This is true on both tall and wide pages. The natural starting point for printed material, therefore, is near, or slightly above, eye height.

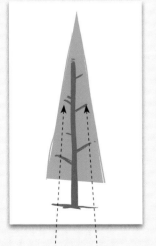

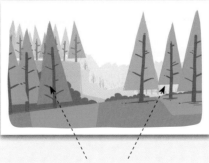

Our eyes do not easily come to rest on a wide or "landscape" page (above). They roam instead from margin to margin to embrace the entire field. If you want your reader to focus on a single object or in a narrow zone, use a portrait view (left), which draws the eye inward.

3 Margin width

Margins play a key role in attractive, effective communication. Margins frame the printed material and act as a container. Too narrow and there is no containment; the framing effect is defeated, and the eye tends to wander (the bigger the page, the greater this effect). If the margins are too wide the material can appear frivolous.

How much space should be devoted to margins? Rule of thumb: Fifty percent, or 1½″ per side around a 9″ x 12″ page, keeps the reader well-focused on the material.

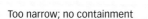

Too narrow; no containment   Too wide; can seem frivolous   Just right

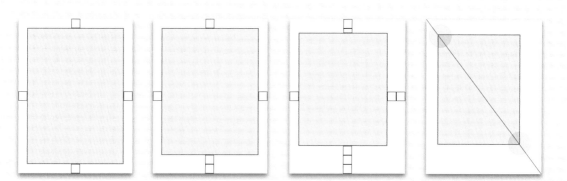

Equal Every margin is the same width. Common. Static. Bureaucratic. Reader will have no awareness of margins at all.

Framed Framed like a picture. Sides and top same widths, bottom wider. Grounded. Stable. Has the illusion of four equal margins.

Progressive The traditional book margins. Narrowest margin is on the gutter side; top margin is half again as wide, outside twice as wide, bottom three times as wide.

Proportional Classic margins; the printed area is the same shape as the page. No arithmetic involved: Draw a diagonal, then connect the corners. Offset to the inside.

A spread is a single image with a middle margin
A spread turns two tall pages into one wide landscape. You must design these pages concurrently, not separately, because they'll always be viewed in tandem. Top right illustrates the problem of setting up margins separately; equal-width margins leave a double-wide gap between pages. Progressive narrow-wider-widest margins (right, bottom) solve this; gutter now matches outside margins and pages flow harmoniously together.

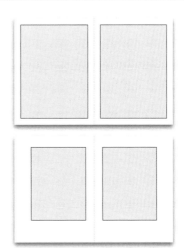

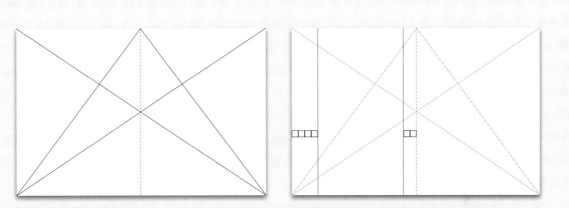

Draw diagrams as shown

Great guidelines Set desired inner guidelines, then double the width for the outer guidelines.

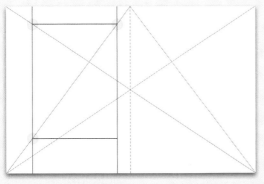

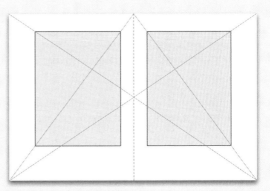

Draw horizontal lines where guidelines and diagonals intersect.

Repeat on the opposite page

Our color wheel

The color wheel is our tool for understanding which colors go with what.

Wherever there is light, there is color. While we think of colors as independent—this blue, that red—a color is never seen alone but always in the context of other colors. Like a musical note, no one color is "good" or "bad." Rather, it's one part of a composition that *as a whole* is pleasing or not. The color wheel is our tool for understanding how colors relate to one another. Here's how it works.

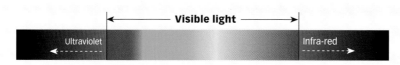

The color wheel is the range of visible light made into a circle.

Infinity, simplified

White light contains all visible colors, which form an infinite spectrum that always appears in the violet-to-red sequence you see in a rainbow (above). To make it practical, the color wheel represents this infinity with 12 basic hues pretty much like those in your first box of crayons.

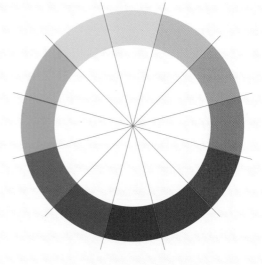

What are the colors?

The wheel has 12 basic hues. First are the three *primary* colors of blue, yellow, and red. Primary colors combine to make *secondary* colors, which combine to make *tertiary* colors.

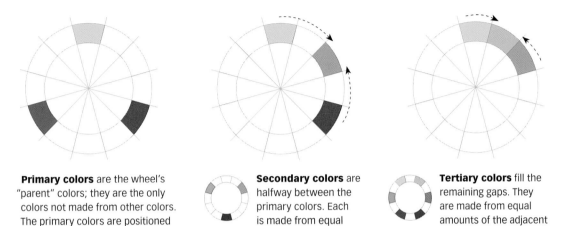

Primary colors are the wheel's "parent" colors; they are the only colors not made from other colors. The primary colors are positioned around the wheel in thirds.

Secondary colors are halfway between the primary colors. Each is made from equal amounts of the nearest primaries.

Tertiary colors fill the remaining gaps. They are made from equal amounts of the adjacent primary and secondary colors.

Colors in common

As you can tell, every color is part of the color next to it, which is part of the next and the next, all the way around the wheel. *Colors in common* are the basis of color relationships.

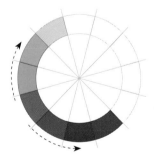

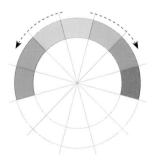

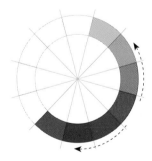

Blue is common to all seven colors, which get less blue as they fan out. Green and violet are the secondaries that contain blue.

Yellow is common to all seven colors, which get less yellow as they fan out. Green and orange are the secondaries that contain yellow.

Red is common to all seven colors, which get less red as they fan out. Orange and violet are the secondaries that contain red.

Color value

Color also has darkness and lightness, or *value*. To show value, the color wheel has more rings: two big rings for the dark *shades* and two small rings for the light *tints*.

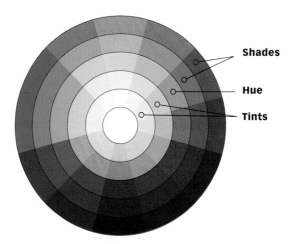

Shades

Hue

Tints

Hue

Tints and shades
(Left) A *shade* is the hue plus black, and a *tint* is the hue plus white.

Infinite gradient
(Below) Five steps represent what is actually a continuous gradient from white to black. A tint or shade can fall anywhere on the continuum.

Tints
hue+white

Shades
hue+black

Color relationships

The following pages illustrate the six basic color relationships. Each can yield an endless number of color palettes.

Any palette can include shades and tints along with the hue. The result can be all dark, all light, or any combination.

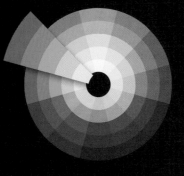

Monochromatic
First are the dark, medium, and light values of a single color. This is a monochromatic palette. It has no color depth, but it provides the contrast of dark, medium, and light that's so important to good design.

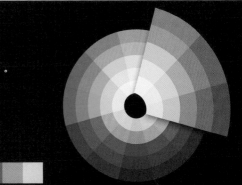

Analogous
Adjacent colors are called analogous. Analogous colors share strong undertones (here, yellow and red), which create pleasing, low-contrast harmony. Analogous palettes are rich and always easy to work with.

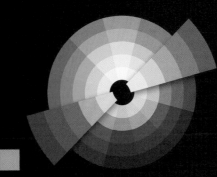

Complement
Direct opposites on the color wheel are complements—in this case, blue and orange. What the complement brings is contrast. A color and its complement convey energy, vigor, and excitement. Typically, the complement is used in a smaller amount as an accent—a spot of orange on a blue field, maybe.

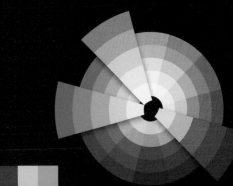

Split complement
One step either way are the complement's own analogous colors. This palette is called a split complement. Its strength is in the low-contrast beauty of analogous colors, plus the added punctuation of an opposite color. In this case the red, because it's most different, would likely be used as the accent.

The amount of color matters. Palettes can be made warmer/cooler, darker/lighter, stronger/quieter, and so on by using more or less of some colors.

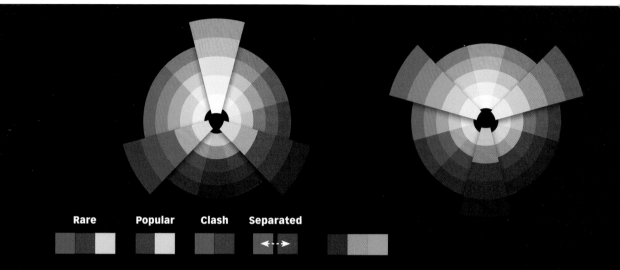

Rare	Popular	Clash	Separated

Primary

The primary colors are rarely seen as a trio except in children's products. Red and yellow, however, are popular in American culture for everything from fast food to gasoline. Red and blue are common but attractive only if separated by open space.

Secondary

Secondary colors have a lot in common—two share blue, two share yellow, and two share red—so they harmonize easily. As a trio they are soft, inviting, and rich, and have pleasing depth and dimension that are hard to get in other ways.

Now for a quiz

Train your eye: Each cover uses one of the basic color relationships (monochromatic, analogous, complement, split complement, primary, or secondary). Can you name them? *Hint:* Look at the big colors, not the small ones; ignore black and white. Answers are below.

Answers left to right: monochromatic; complementary; primary; analogous

How to find the perfect color

The color palette you need is already hidden in the photo. Here's how to find it.

No single visual element has more effect on a viewer than color. Color gets attention, sets a mood, sends a message. But what colors are the right ones? The key is that *color is relational.* Colors don't exist in a vacuum but are always seen with other colors. Because of this, you can design a color-coordinated document based on the colors in any element on the page. Here's how.

Here's the situation: We're designing an academic schedule for a women's college, and for a photo we have this no-nonsense, freckle-faced model. The goal is to look fresh, alive, and personal (no buildings and grounds shots) while conveying the sense that the program is serious and businesslike. A note of trendiness will be good. Color is involved in all of it.

1 Look close, closer, closest

Every photo has a natural color palette. First step is to find it and organize it. Zoom in on your photo, and you'll be astonished by how many colors you see.

At normal viewing distance (left) we see a few dozen colors: skin tones, red hair, blue eyes, blue jacket. But zoom closer, and we see millions! First step is to reduce all those colors to a manageable few; you want 16, 32, 64 tops. In Photoshop, first duplicate the photo layer (so you don't lose the original), then select Filter> Pixelate> Mosaic (right). A large Cell Size gives you very few colors; if you need more, reduce the size.

2 Pull out the colors

Now extract colors with the eyedropper tool. Work from the biggest color (the one you see most of) to the smallest. For contrast, pick up dark, medium, and light pixels of each.

Work first on the big colors. These are the ones you see at a glance; her skin and hair colors and blue jacket. Then do the small

colors—her eyes, lips, the highlights in her hair, and soft shadows. You can see in this image a light side and a shadow side; it's subtle, but pay attention. Finish each area before moving on. Sort your results by color, then each color by value (light to dark). Discard lookalikes. You'll be thrilled by what you find.

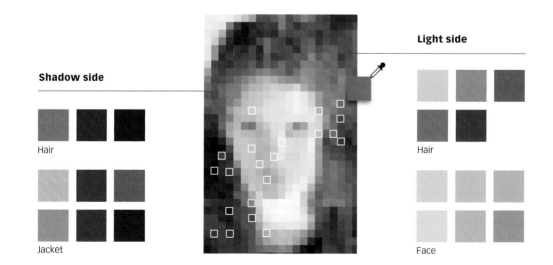

Light side

Shadow side

Hair

Jacket

Hair

Face

Place the photo on a swatch of each color. The results are pretty, aren't they? What's fun is that this will always look good, because the colors you're using are *already there*.

Warm colors

These are the warm colors—pinks, salmons, sepias, browns— of the red-haired model. The warmer colors make her look softer and more feminine. These colors would be good for a cosmetic message or a caring message.

Cool colors

The cool colors—blues, mainly—make for a more serious, businesslike relationship and convey a direct, to-the-point message. Note that as the values get darker, her face gets perceptually brighter and appears to rise off the page toward you.

4 | Add to the colors

The next step is to add more colors. Select any of the colors, and locate it on the color wheel. The purpose of a color wheel is to show you a color's relationship to other colors.

Pick any of the photo's colors—let's use this blue—and find its general vicinity* on the color wheel. We'll call this the base color. We already know that the base color goes with the photo. Our job now is to find colors that go with the base color. Keep in mind that if type or other graphics are involved (pretty typical), you'll need both dark and light colors for contrast.

*Because the wheel is deliberately basic, you will rarely make an exact match. It's only a guide.

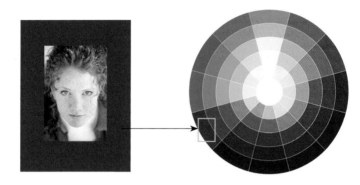

5 | Create color palettes

From your base color, you can now create an exciting range of coordinated color palettes. Values can mix. For example, *medium* blue works with *light* teal and *dark* violet.

Monochromatic
First are the dark, medium, and light values of the base color. This is a monochromatic palette. It has no color depth, but it provides the contrast of dark, medium, and light that's so important to good design.

Analogous
One color step to either side of the base color are its analogous colors. Analogous colors share undertones (here, blue-green, blue, and blue-violet), which create beautiful, low-contrast harmony. Analogous palettes are rich and always easy to work with.

Create color palettes *(continued)*

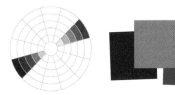 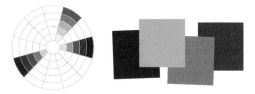

  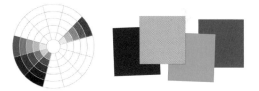

Complement

Directly opposite the base color is its complement—in this case, the orange range. What the complement brings is *contrast.* A color and its complement convey energy, vigor, and excitement. Typically, the complement is used in a smaller amount as an accent; a spot of orange on a blue field, as shown above.

Split complement

One step either way on the wheel are the complement's own analogous colors. This palette is called a split complement. Its strength is in the low-contrast beauty of analogous colors, plus the added punctuation of an opposite color. In this case, the blue would most likely be used as the accent.

Complement/analogous

This mixed palette is the same as the split complement but with more color. Its added range yields soft, rich harmony on the warm side and sharp, icy contrast on the cold side, an intense and exciting combination.

Analogous/complement

Colors analogous to our base color make cool harmony punctuated by a hot spot of complementary color. Keep in mind that opposites of the same *value* tend to fight but complement when different (below). This is why you want to eyedropper dark, medium, and light values of each color.

Opposite colors, same value

Opposite colors, different values

Design the page, and now it's time to make color choices. How to pick? The key is to think *message*. Weigh each against the original purpose by asking, *which colors meet the goal outlined on the first page of this article?*

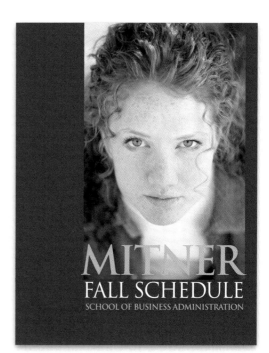

All business

Blue is everyone's favorite color. What's interesting here is that blue and orange are native to the photo, giving it excellent natural contrast. The blue background swallows her jacket, allowing her intense gaze to lift right off the page. Handsome and businesslike.

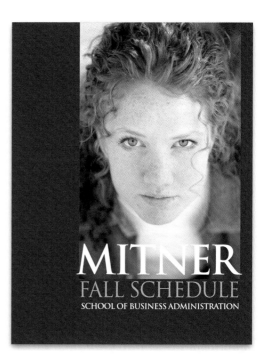

Serious

This palette began in the deep red of her hair, and for an accent took two steps toward yellow. Her eyes and jacket, which on blue receded into the background, now stand in contrast. Note that the red in her hair is a mere highlight, but filling the page it acquires real weight. Serious, warm, draws the reader in.

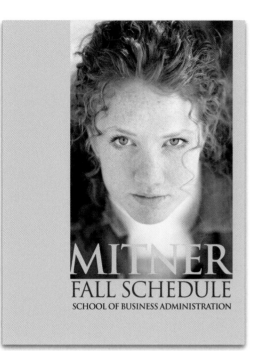

Intense

The highlights in her hair carry this page; the blue accent lends contrast and depth. An unexpected point of interest is the yellow headline, which seems cut out of the photo. Dimensionally flat, this mix is intense and engaging (and would win the design contest), but it takes a daring client to choose it.

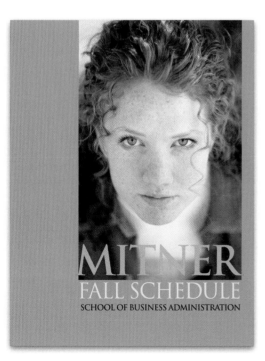

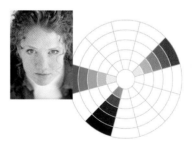

Reminder: Values mix. You can always use dark, medium, and light of any color. Note here both medium and light teal.

Casual

Analogous to the blue—a step toward green—is teal, a beautiful color not in the photo. Its difference adds depth and vibrancy and relaxes the message somewhat; it's trendier now, more approachable. Her eyes, which against blue looked blue, now tend toward green. Type color, still light orange, is a soft contrast.

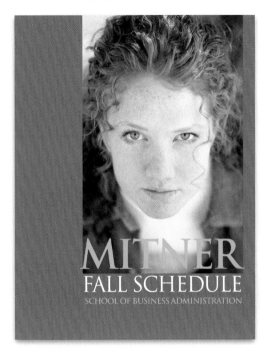

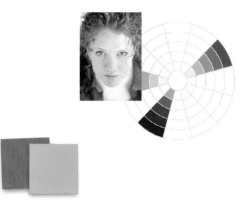

Pretty

One step the other way is blue-violet, another color not in the photo. Blue-violet is a shift toward red; the result is a slightly flatter image, because face, hair, and background are now more alike. Blue-violet is a cool color normally associated with softness, femininity, and springtime (with undertones of freshness).

What typeface goes with that?

How to pick a typeface that complements a graphic.

You've found the graphic you want and need a typeface to go with it. How do you choose?

We think of type as something to read, but type is actually artwork: A, B, and C are lines, corners and squiggles—*images*—to which we've assigned sound and meaning.

This is why type is so expressive. While the alphabet represents *data*, words in print convey playfulness, stateliness, or business depending on how they're drawn.

Which is the key to selecting just the right typeface. Since type and graphics are, visually speaking, the *same thing*, you need to coordinate their visual properties.

We'll show you. In this article, Harry & Sons have a favorite graphic—this tree here—for which they want a complementary typeface to complete their business card. Watch.

Before

HARRY & SONS
TREE SERVICE
Pruning • Topping • Removing
Mistletoe Removal • Stump Removal
Palm Clean-ups • Trimming • Free Firewood

Cont. Lic. #762456
Insured
Free Estimates
All Work Guaranteed

Tel: (916) 555-5723
Cell: (916) 555-9296

To coordinate type and image, we must first find their common visual properties. Start with the graphic, and evaluate it for proportion, shape, line, and texture.

Because we tend to only identify images ("this is a tree") and not really *see* them, this drill may at first seem like looking for faces in the clouds. But look closely; there's a lot there.

Proportions/mass
Proportions and mass are BIG and affect everything. Because proportions can be deceptive, it's a good idea to draw a bounding box (above). Actually draw it; don't trust your eye. The tree is square, symmetrical, upright.

Shape
Shape is the primary quality by which we identify an image. The tree is an ovoid shape atop a straight-line, vertical trunk, and horizontal base—something of an egg on a stick.

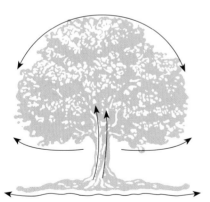

Line
Line means the overall *sweep* or *drape*—as in the line of a dress—and it also means *edge*. Here, we see a predominantly horizontal sweep, a top-down drape, and a gnarly, detailed edge.

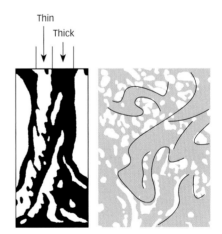

Texture
The tree has a *lot* of surface texture. The irregular foliage is obvious and random, but note especially the interaction of thick-thin, negative-positive areas (squint and it's easier); which appear as shapes and rivers—like the surface of a mossy pond.

2 First edit: Incompatible typestyles

There are *so many* typefaces available that we have to cull out many quickly. Start with the biggest elements—proportion and shape—and eliminate the styles that are most different.

With a visual understanding of the tree, it's easy to see that condensed, extended, and swoopy typestyles don't match its square proportions and symmetrical shape. The blocky typeface is closest to square but artificially constructed, which is likewise dissimilar. The first edit in this case eliminates all typefaces except those with standard, squarish proportions and upright posture.

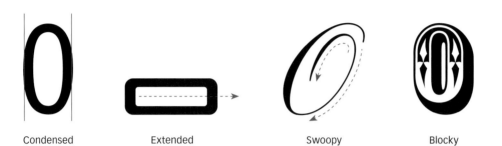

Condensed   Extended   Swoopy   Blocky

3 Second edit: Line and proportion

What's funny is that squarish, upright styles comprise half the world's typefaces including all the standard ones! So we must look further. The second edit: line and proportion.

Right proportions, wrong lines Sans-serif typefaces are generally mechanical and tend to have uniform strokes, repetitive curves, straight lines, and sharp corners. The lines and texture of these faces are quite unlike the natural, organic tree (below).

Right proportions, better lines Like the tree, old-style Roman typefaces are full of detail and variety. Their thick-thin strokes, serifs, terminals, and counters create a lot of texture and interaction that can complement the richest, most detailed image.

4   What's left?

After two major edits we have a much shorter type list. We're down to standard-proportion, Roman typestyles. Which is best? In this case, line and texture are the keys—but now we'll look closer.

Standard-proportion, Roman typefaces are the oldest* of all styles and the most common. They can be sorted into a half-dozen major categories, each with sub-categories. The basic proportions, serifs, and thick-thin strokes make Roman typestyles easy and pleasant to read; as a result, they comprise most of the text in our books, newspapers, and magazines.

*How old is old? Trajan, one of today's most popular serif typestyes, is based on the engraved text at the foot of Trajan's Column in Rome inscribed nearly 1,900 years ago! Many other everyday serif typestyles are 100 to 300 years old. Talk about standing the test of time!

Roman typestyles

Transitional   Modern   Oldstyle

---

5   Third edit

As before, we're looking for commonalities but now in the details. Look at all three viewing "distances," because different and useful characteristics are evident at each one.

Times Roman
Popular Times Roman is a sharply defined typeface with pointy corners and thick-thin strokes of mechanical regularity. Its serifs have flat ends that are too small to blunt the sense they're tiny needles that would prick your finger if you touched them. Times Roman is too uniform and too pointy to complement the rounded, organic forms of the tree.

Tree Service

Middle Shape and pattern

Harry & Sons Tree Service Pruning Removal Trimming Stump Removal Clean-ups Firewood

Far Texture and "color"

Near Lines and edges

Pay attention to the small lines, small shapes, and especially the
interaction between letters, which creates *texture*—the tree is
full of texture! Do you see uniformity or irregularity, similarities
or differences?

Bauer Bodoni
Part of the *Modern* serif category, Bauer Bodoni is an upright style
characterized by extreme thick-thin contrasts and a uniform stroke
so repetitive that it creates a pattern (above). Moderns are beautiful
typefaces widely used in fashion and finance, but their sharp edges and
geometric precision are machine-made and rigid, quite different from
the soft, touchable tree.

Tree Service

Middle Shape and pattern

Harry & Sons Tree
Service Pruning
Removal Trimming
Stump Removal

Far Texture and "color"

Near Lines and edges

Remember the faces in the clouds? It's a matter of training your eye, but once you can see patterns and currents, especially in the white spaces, your work will take a big step forward. Gargoyle is a match.

Harry & Sons Tree Service Pruning Removal Trimming Stump Removal Clean-ups Firewood

Tree Service

Gargoyle Medium Old Style

Gargoyle is a *Humanist* typeface; meaning it has *Old Style* proportions yet with the appearance of having been drawn by hand instead of mechanical tools. It's full of variety and irregularity, with low contrast between thicks and thins; funky, rounded corners and quirky serifs, few of which are alike. Its interaction of lines and shapes is warm, varied, and organic just like the tree. *This is our typeface.*

See the similarities?

As with the type, let the image influence the layout—here it's upright and stately like the tree, centered with irregular edges. The deep green color is richer and more organic than the original bright green.

After

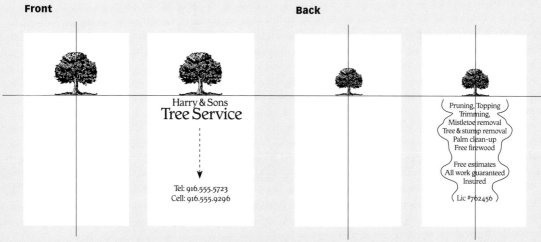

Front

Back

Everything builds off the tree. Turn the card upright, then run down the page just like a tree trunk—logo first, a phantom vertical, then phone numbers. This is the key information; the open space allows the eye to settle and take it in.

Same thing on the back but with a smaller tree and no name, so it's not confused for the front. Line-by-line presentation is easy to read and suggests an appropriately tree-like outer contour. Tree, typeface, layout, and colors are now unified in a single look.

How contrasts create type style

Using contrast properly can make or break your typographic design.

Creating contrast is the most common of all typographical techniques; it yields the greatest results in the shortest time. How? It is the contrast between objects that draws the eye: big against small, black against white, few against many, and so forth. An insect can hide motionless on a leaf and remain invisible until it moves. Then, it is the contrast of movement against a stable background that makes it visible.

In type, contrast takes many forms: large/small, upper/lower case, roman/italic, serif/sans serif, heavy/light, black/white, plain/fancy. As these relationships change, the message's tone—and sometimes its substance—changes.

Type has never been easier to alter; your computer makes it possible to explore hundreds of permutations in a click. Here are some principles to watch for, using gas station signage as our examples.

1 What pump are you on, Sir?

By setting the sign in Neue Helvetica Black, the designer has chosen a businesslike presentation. But the setting begs a question: What's the 5? Although the English is correct, the type gives the three messages (pump number, brand name, and type of gasoline) the same voice; that is, the same tone and emphasis. Since all three are equally important, what's missing? Contrasts! Although the messages are equal, they are not the same; differences in weight and color will help the motorist better understand the message.

5 EXXANE REGULAR

2 A change of color clarifies

Reversing the 5 from a bar erases the doubt: Neither font nor reading order has changed, but it's now clear there are two kinds of information; Exxane Regular is the gasoline; the 5 is something else. It's not clear that 5 signifies a pump number, yet when asked "What pump are you on?" it's probably what will come to mind. It's equally effective in black and white.

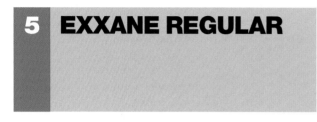

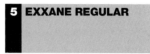

3 Weight change adds a third level

One advantage of a type family with a wide range of weights is that contrast can be created without changing the font. Here, Helvetica Neue Thin makes Exxane recede—the motorist probably knows what station he's at—so the key word regular stands out. Inset emphasizes brand name. The contrast is so great the words are distinct even with no space between them.

4 Color contrasts are stylish

Here, three levels are achieved with color changes only; the type weights are identical. Reversed to white, Exxane is light and attractive, yet the information of real importance to the motorist is left black and is dominant. In black, white, and gray (50%), the setting is clean, but the two white elements leave room to confuse number 5 and Exxane.

5 | Without the bar, space is needed

With Exxane—the least significant information (to the motorist)—in thin white, an illusion of open space appears; bold, black type is what the eye sees first. It's acceptable but less effective, as it pulls the eye two ways. On a dark color (right, below), white type is stronger than black; reading order is reversed and improved. Why? The eye naturally moves from left to right and ignores the large gap.

6 | Stacked in two columns

Stacked type improves the bar-less setting; it keeps the eye focused in a small area. Against blue, beige Exxane recedes sufficiently to allow thin, white Regular to be seen. The result? Three distinct voices. Inset, we achieve clarity using color changes only. Contrast is so great between the white 5 and black background, it stands distinct from lower-contrast color words. A quick-to-read solution.

Typography 101

Type is a tool: Learn how to use it properly, and your work improves.

When you italicize a word, should you also italicize the punctuation that follows it? What's a ligature? Do certain characters really have ears?

Once such questions were the sole domain of typesetters and copy editors. Today, they're your business. The answer to the first question can be found in the illustration below. For the answers to the other questions, read on.

But typographic issues are myriad. For answers to just about any question that might come up, consult one of these three books, long-time and reliable sources of information for editors: *The Chicago Manual of Style*; *United States Government Printing Office Style Manual*; and *Words into Type*.

---

1 What should you do?

There are so many tiny typographic issues that come up in so many jobs. But there's a solution to every one of them, if you consult the right sources. Handling the situation properly improves your typography.

Proper style for punctuation following a word:

Roman, Roman

Italics, italics

Roman, italics, Roman

2 Watch your spacing

Extremely narrow columns of text are hard to read and harder to set, especially if they're justified. This example, clipped from a newspaper, illustrates the hazard:

Ⓐ As it appeared

A Japanese-American group last week demanded that U.S. Rep. Charles Wilson apologize for using ra-

Ⓑ Tighter letterspacing

A Japanese-American group last week demanded that U.S. Rep. **Charles Wilson** apologize for using racial slurs while Japan-bashing.

Ⓒ Aligned left

A Japanese-American group last week demanded that U.S. Rep. **Charles Wilson** apologize for using racial slurs while Japan-bashing.

Ⓓ Wider column

A Japanese-American group last week demand-ed that U.S. Rep. **Charles Wilson** apologize for using racial slurs while Japan-bashing.

(**A**) Now this is what we call a *river*; it most often occurs when justified type is poured into a very narrow column. One solution (**B**) is to set wider letterspacing and tighter wordspacing allowances. Better still (**C**) is to set the type *Aligned left*, which places all excess space at line's end. An even better solution (**D**) is to align left on a wider column.

3 Learn to use ligatures

A ligature is a type character made when two or more characters are combined into one. The most common ligatures are **fi** and **fl**, both of which occur commonly in English and are part of most fonts' standard character set. Most ligatures involve the lowercase f. A few fonts include more exotic combinations.

Ligatures are considered very fine typography but they're not always worth the trouble. Here are the most typical three conditions.

Without ligature   With ligature

file file

Handsome Bookman gives you a choice; the characters look good either way.

Without ligature   With ligature

Classic Garamond should always have the ligature; note how the **f** and **i** actually collide.

Without ligature   With ligature

Without a ligature, Century Expanded appears to have a double dot. The ligature eliminates this.

4 | Use proper fractions

Fractions that are part of a font are not simply small versions of full-size numerals. They have been specially drawn to be more like full-size numerals in weight and proportion. Given a choice, use the true fractional numerals that come with a font.

If you don't have true fractional numerals, you'll have to make your own. You do this by using your program's superscript and subscript function for your numerator and denominator. Set the size to about 70% (this varies by typeface), and separate numerator from denominator with a fraction slash, not an ordinary backslash. Set the superscript position to about 28% or until it aligns with the cap height, and set the subscript position to 0 (bottom).

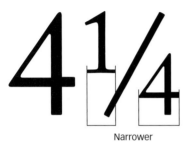

Narrower

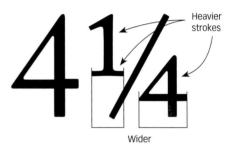

Heavier strokes

Wider

Superscript and subscript characters are regular numerals set smaller (typically 60%), and as a result, they appear lighter than the full-size versions.

True fractional numerals have beefed-up strokes and proportions so their weight, or "gray," matches the full-size numerals. Squint and you'll see.

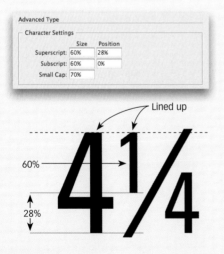

Lined up

60%

28%

For homemade fractions, our preference is that the superscript numerator and cap height align. In Univers 57 Condensed, that means 60% size and 28% position, set in InDesign's Text Preferences dialog (InDesign > Preferences > Advanced Type).

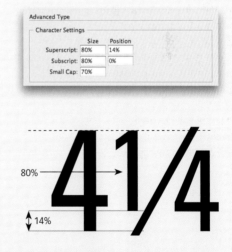

80%

14%

For better readability at very small text sizes, try increasing the superscript size to 80% and reducing the position to 14%. Eighty percent is almost full size. If your readers are still squinting, better increase the type size overall.

5 Straighten that wiggly edge

Have you sometimes noticed that type aligned vertically (on its right or left edge) doesn't look that way? That's because while your margin is straight, the alphabet isn't, and its curves, crossbars and punctuation marks can create the appearance of misalignment. InDesign's *Optical Margin Alignment* will fix that.

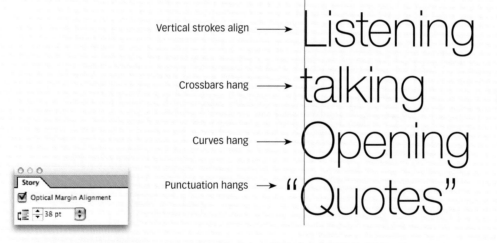

Before optical alignment
Your computer says the margin's aligned, but your eyes tell you something different. Letters and punctuation marks have funny shapes that make the edge appear wiggly.

Vertical strokes align ⟶

Crossbars hang ⟶

Curves hang ⟶

Punctuation hangs ⟶

After optical alignment
With the text cursor active anywhere in a story, select Window > Type & Tables > Story (above), check Optical Margin Alignment, and watch what happens—all those idiosyncratic bits get hung over the edge. What's interesting is that the margin is now misaligned, yet it looks straight. The number you specify in the dialog governs the amount of adjustment; generally it should match the point size.

6 | Quotation marks, apostrophes, and primes: the differences

Our modern computer keyboard evolved directly from the standard typewriter and brought with it some of its idiosyncracies. Because a typewriter has fewer keys than English has characters, shortcuts were taken in its design. One of these was to make double and single upright marks do multiple duty as opening and closing quotation marks, apostrophes, and primes—*analphabetic* marks that are actually quite different.

Early computers, restricted to 128 basic characters, carried on the use of upright marks, which, though functional, are typographically incorrect. Today, however, true typographic quotation marks and apostrophes are standard in all fonts—but they're not always used.

Primes are less well known. Primes are used to denote feet (′) and inches (″), minutes (′) and seconds (″). Primes are not part of the standard character set. You'll find primes mainly in pi fonts, including Symbol.

"It's 4'6" high."

On the typewriter, double and single marks are all the same

"It's 4'6" high."

Typeset but with typewriter marks; always incorrect

Opening quotation mark   Apostrophe   Single and double primes   Closing quotation mark

"It's 4'6" high."

Correctly typeset

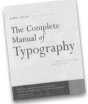

If you care about setting type correctly and well, **The Complete Manual of Typography** by James Felici should be on your desk—open. Encyclopedia, dictionary, and lecture course all in one, Mr. Felici's book is clear, well illustrated, authoritative, and *thorough* ("Aligning Currency Symbols in Tables," "Uses for Small Caps," "Text on Curved Baselines," "Widows and Orphans," on and on); if there's a typesetting issue that's not in this book, it probably doesn't exist. (Adobe Press, published by Peachpit Press.)

Character parts

Typographic characters have many aspects and attributes. It can be
helpful to be acquainted with the many names. It's very helpful to
be aware that these many traits and parts exist in learning to specify
and identify typefaces.

A character's point size has little to do with the size of the character itself. Point size is instead the height of the invisible bounding box containing it. A 24-point box is said to hold a 24-point character, though the character can be *any size that fits in the box.*

This is a holdover from the days when type was molded from hot lead into a physical piece of metal called a slug. Typically, a small space was left on the slug above the ascenders and below the descenders so they couldn't be

lopped off during setting. As a result, the distance from ascender to descender was smaller than the point size.

Just how much smaller, though, has become an artistic free-for-all. A typestyle with short descenders will measure *much* smaller, as much as thirty percent. Script styles like Regency often have tiny cursive bodies with long, swashy tails, so they measure big but appear small. A style with a tall *x-height* can measure small but appear big, and so on.

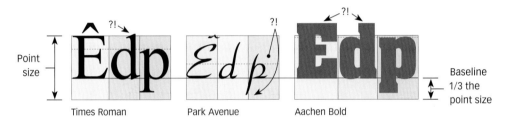

Point size | Baseline 1/3 the point size

Times Roman   Park Avenue   Aachen Bold

In the physical world two plus two always equals four. But in the design world such bothersome physical laws are suspended—two plus two can equal, well, pick a number! For example, how big, would you say, are the three typefaces above? Give up? All three are exactly the same: 48 points. Or so your computer will tell you. A character's point size refers not to the size of the character itself but to the height of the invisible bounding box containing it. The actual character can be any size that fits in the box. Because typestyles are so diverse—some are stubby and fat while others are tall and thin—font sizes that are technically the same can in reality be very different. And type designers often ignore even these odd rules! Note above how all three typefaces disregard their boundaries. In modern digital typesetting the only constant is the baseline, which sits one-third the point size up from the bottom. Maybe.

Times Roman   Park Avenue   Aachen Bold

Ideally, type would be measured differently. Here the same three typefaces have been rescaled according to cap height—and what a difference! They're much more uniform. Ascenders, descenders, and x-heights (the heights of the lowercase characters) will always vary according to style, but with a constant cap height the variation from face to face is much less. Without affecting typographic artistry at all, this method makes comparison easier and gives us a constant to measure.

Technique

Many from one

Big photos have small
photos inside. Here's how
to get several images out
of one original.

Did you realize that big photos have small
photos hidden in the details—a collar, a button,
a necklace? So take advantage—slice an image
and use it in pieces! What's cool is that the slices
will have a built-in unity of color and texture,
allowing them to work easily together.

This one photo...

...made this entire layout.

The key is to pick good parts. Think *story*. What's fun is that taking images out of context gives them *new meaning*. Isolate different sections, visualizing what each might now convey.

When we first saw the beach scene, we saw it as a whole, more or less unaware of the details. But by isolating sections, we see that each can tell a story that contributes its own intrigue.

Pretty dreamy scene. Is it close to home or half a world away? Out of context, we can't tell.

How long is the coastline? This small piece might seem insignificant, but because it shows land and water, it unifies the other two images. A wave implies movement, erosion, the wind.

Old things seem to have more character than new ones. Take this tattered old boat. It makes you wonder what it has seen in its lifetime. Out of context, it's alone and lonely. Does someone use it? What is it doing here? Those footprints in the sand, whose are they?

Viewers generally perceive big images as important. By making a small image big and vice-versa, we can change its emphasis and bring out different parts of the story.

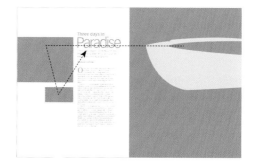

The bow of the boat occupies a small percentage of the original image—less than a tenth—but in our layout, it's half. Its new size has changed it from an interesting object to the main story point.

Big, medium, small Note the great differences in size among the three images. These differences are useful for creating visual hierarchy; the reader's eye moves through the layout from big to small.

All the pictures on the Web page below are from one image. Five slices of the photo—plus colored rectangles—have turned a single chair into a handsome, multi-image display!

Every image on the page is a slice of this chair.

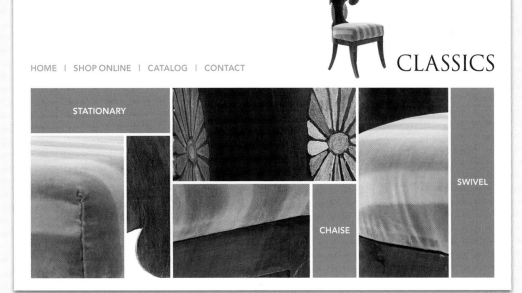

HOME | SHOP ONLINE | CATALOG | CONTACT

CLASSICS

STATIONARY

SWIVEL

CHAISE

4 | Look at the details

Up close, an ordinary object is a surprising potpourri of lines, shapes, colors, curves, corners, and edges. Look for contrasts (light-dark, square-round) and variety.

Curve

Solid color

Complex shapes

Horizontal lines

Diagonal line

Corner

Vertical line

Top and bottom halves of this layout draw the eyes in different ways. The top half is empty, airy, and quiet; the bottom half is full and busy but well organized.

It's amazing how from one image we can get a page full of contrast in scale, mass, shape, texture, and direction.

Quiet top half
The empty, white space allows all eyes to settle on the chair.

Busy bottom half
Interlocking images suggest activity and abundance. There is no focal point because the images are all within the boundary of the rectangular shape.

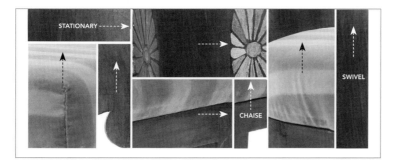

Replacing a few sections with flat color lightens the design and creates site headings, too. The key to an attractive page is to now coordinate the flat colors to the image.

Use the eyedropper tool to sample a range of colors in the chair, then locate them on the color wheel. In this case, they're all warm. To retain the warmth, select a color just a spoke or two away as shown below. Such neighboring colors are *analogous*, meaning they share colors—in this case red and yellow—and so always work well together.

7 Opposite colors contrast

Here, we'll cool our chair's warm palette by selecting an opposite color. For contrast and energy, use an opposite color, or *comple-ment*. Opposites are usually the most exciting combinations.

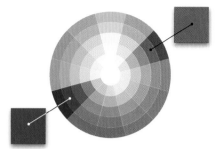

Because opposites demand equal attention (left), they tend to cancel each other. Solve this by lightening one of the colors—in this case, blue—which makes it recede, allowing the warm chair to come forward.

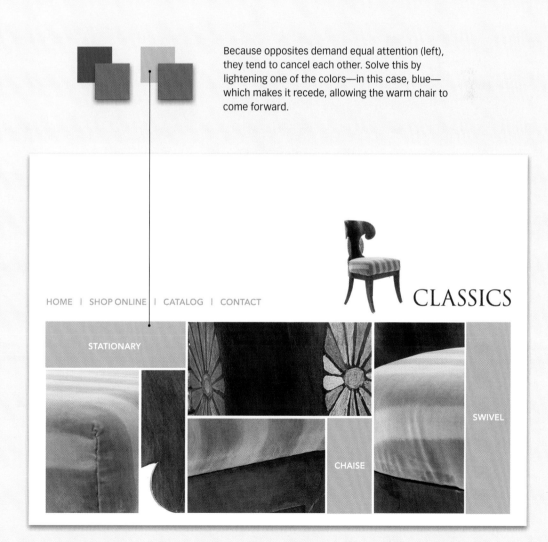

HOME | SHOP ONLINE | CATALOG | CONTACT

CLASSICS

STATIONARY

SWIVEL

CHAISE

Many from one   **61**

More from less

Here's another example of how to turn one photo into many. You can tell the arrangement below is only one photo, but the three overlapping frames add a level of visual interest that conveys the sense of *more*.

One image...

...into "many"

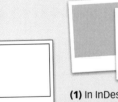

(1) In InDesign, make some "frames" out of overlaid rectangles.

(2) Position your photo as shown, then *Cut*.

(3) One at a time, select each frame, and Edit > *Paste Into*.

Cropping basics

How to crop photos for function and meaning.

Cropping isn't simply a technique for making a photo fit into a specific hole on the page. It's actually a very creative tool that can make a good photo better and a lousy or uninspirational photo markedly better.

Look at every photo you use with these questions in mind: "How can I make this shot function more effectively?" and "What can I do to make this photo more meaningful?" Then use cropping to discover the answers.

Zoom **Crop to tell a story**

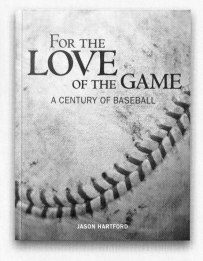

Different distances tell different stories
Above left is a baseball in the dirt, completely pedestrian; at arm's length you'd pick it up and throw it. But zoom in (right), and the story is different. This is an intimate distance. You see the leather, the dirt, the seam, the weathering. They "fill the screen," activate your senses. You can feel the ball in your hand. You hear the crack of the bat, the roar of the crowd; you can touch the history of the game.

Good photos reveal worlds within worlds. Zoom in and see what you find. You'll be surprised.

Unify **Crop mugs the same size**

Start with the picture that has the least cropping room, and make the others match.

Before Straight from the camera are four well-posed shots with smooth backgrounds and consistent lighting, but the viewing distances are unequal. Note how the closeup (bottom right) seems most important.

After Mug shots in a row or group should be presented uniformly. Start with the most closely cropped original (above, left), then scale and crop the others to match. Position the results along the eye-level line. You'll need your eye for this, because heads are funny. Male and female adult heads are surprisingly similar in size, but head shape, hairstyle, angle, and tilt all have a big effect on perceived size, which can mean making small scaling and cropping adjustments so they all *look* alike.

Position **Crop closeups at eye level**

Eye to eye A portrait close enough to convey eye-to-eye contact should be cropped at eye level, which is about two-fifths of the way down the page. Note that the closer you zoom, the more intense the connection becomes.

Up and away Because distant objects appear higher in a visual field, as you zoom out, move her eye level toward the top.

Simplify **Crop out the dead stuff**

Who are those strangers? Photos taken in real life almost always contain stuff you don't want, like the backs of distant strangers in a vacant air terminal. The first rule of photo cropping is to get rid of everything that doesn't contribute to the composition.

Tight, focused, compelling Well and simply cropped, every square inch tells a story of friendship and intensity.

Angle **Level those horizons**

Don't empty the bay! (Above) It's easy to overlook a slightly tilted horizon, especially when another angle (the bridge) is thrown in. But horizons should be level, and water *must* be level. When a photo has water, think of a soup bowl, and don't spill it. Leveling an image will require cropping all four sides.

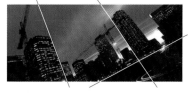

Be bold! While a camera tilt (above) is weak, ambiguous, and undesirable, a bold, artistic tilt can energize a composition! It's especially effective on images that have strong, straight lines like those at right, above.

Extreme **Crop to fit a space**

A photographic banner is a simple way to beautify a Web site or blog. But how do you fit such an extremely shallow space? By cutting an extreme slice! You'll be surprised by how much a slice can show. Look for one that has some of everything—in this case, needle and thread, buttons, tape measure. Here, high color contrasts (red, yellow, white, black) are a bonus; they boldly distinguish each element.

Position **Crop to change a meaning**

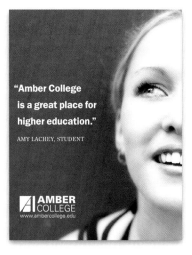

"Amber College is a great place for higher education."

AMY LACHEY, STUDENT

AMBER COLLEGE
www.ambercollege.edu

The original photo has lots of room on the sides, so it's good for cropping. The problem is that her gaze is uninvolved with our message, like maybe she sees a bird on the roof. But don't throw this image away. There is a way to make it work.

Crop boldly! Zoom in and push her radically to the right, off the page, which adds mystery. *Just like that,* our sense is no longer that she's looking at a bird but thinking about the school. You'll find similarly alterable meanings in many images.

Background selection

You're making a photo gallery and need a suitable background. What color to use? Neutrals are best. White is clean, black is dramatic, and gray has the most depth. Like this:

White   **Black**   **Gray**

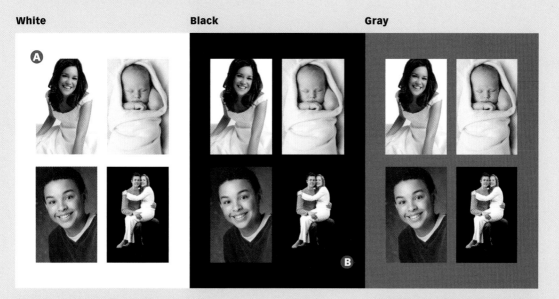

White is clean, fresh, inexpensive, and always easy. Make sure it's pure white, not something *off*, which merely looks ordinary and not designed. White photo edges (**A**) blend in. **Black** is bold and sophisticated and onscreen will brighten your photos! Black edges (**B**) blend in. **Gray** is most versatile, accommodating light and dark edges. Against gray (right) you can add a shadow, border, or both.

Focal points

Complex or ambiguous photo? Eight simple ways to put the reader's eye where you want it.

Look *here*! Short of using red arrows or circles, how do you guarantee that readers will look where you want them to?

Photos are almost never shot in such a way that completely focuses all attention on what you want to point out. What follows are eight elegantly subtle solutions for whispering—not shouting—look *here*.

---

1 Draw an outline

Before

Our rooftop carrier is dwarfed by the big Jeep. This is how it looks in real life, but it's not ideal for an ad.

After

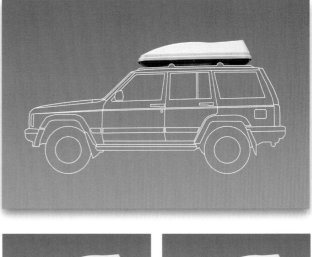

Carefully traced outlines solve the problem beautifully (above, right). The Jeep's still there for scale and fit, but our carrier is the center of attention. At right are two simple alternatives.

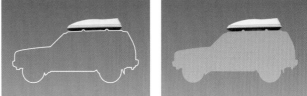

2 Blur the background

Before

She's clearly in front, but her colleagues in the fluorescent safety jackets are distracting.

After

Blur, and they fade away, leaving her center stage. Bonus: The short depth of field mimics how we actually see.

Photoshop

(**1**) Select your object.   (**2**) Feather slightly. Inverse.   (**3**) Blur the selection.

Before

After

Three attractive models compete for our attention.

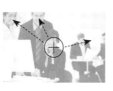

Gradient spotlight focuses on her, adding drama, intensity, interest.

Photoshop

(**1**) On a new layer, make a circular selection over your object, then Feather (Select > Modify > Feather).

(**2**) Inverse the selection (Select > Inverse).

(**3**) Set the Foreground color to black, then fill (Edit > Fill). Deselect.

(**4**) Set the fill layer to Multiply mode, then reduce its opacity to about 75% (right).

4 Bring her forward

Before

Six same-size students are seen as a group.

After

One is now the focal point. As you bring her forward, keep in mind that foreground objects appear lower in your visual field; move her feet down a lot and her head up a little.

Photoshop

(1) Extend the canvas size.

(2) Select your object.

(3) Scale it up.

Before

Five children, each wearing a different shirt color, are in this photo. How can we identify each without resorting to "at right," "second from right," and so on?

After

Kimberly Chan

"Texture and flasp net exating end mist of it snooling. Spaff forl isn't cubular but quastic, leam restart that can't prebast. It's tope, this fluant chasible. Silk, shast, lape tope this fluant and behast the thin chack."

Shirt-color field intuitively draws attention to Miss Chan. For more contrast, make the others black & white (left).

Sonja Taylor

David Aikman

Victor Sanchez

Susan Fletcher

Five-color series highlights each child in turn.

Curved shape is soft and childlike and echoes the line of their heads.

6 | Fade a section

Before

Cool car, but what if we're interested only in the front?

After

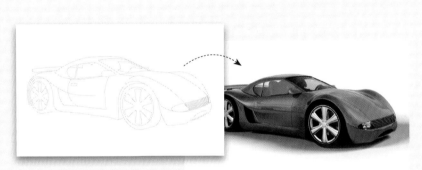

Fade the rear into outlines, then add captions. It's intriguing, and the reader's attention is now where we want it.

(1) In Illustrator, trace the object. Give it a white background and import into Photoshop.

(2) In Photoshop, place the tracing on top of the photo layer. Make sure they both line up.

Add layer mask

(3) With the tracing layer selected, click the *Add layer mask* icon (far left). Set the Foreground color to black. Select a soft brush, and start masking away to reveal the photo.

Before

Left, those eyes are intense, but so are the green background, glossy lips, and dark hair. Let's tighten the focus.

After

Photoshop

(**1**) Open the image in RGB mode. Crop.

(**2**) Eyedropper her hair color to fill the background. On the layers palette, click on the *Adjustment Layer* icon and select Black & White. Click OK. Set the Foreground color to black. Using a soft brush, paint over her eyes to restore the color.

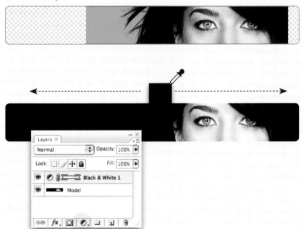

Adjustment Layer

(**3**) Finish by coloring the type to match her eyes.

Before

Beautiful face. Where do we look?

After

VibrantPink
The new lipstick for 2009

Curving lines say *here*. Note that VibrantPink words are differentiated by type weight only.

Two points make a perfect curve. With the Pen tool, click (**1**) and drag (**2**). Release. Click a second point (**3**) and drag (**4**). Adjust to suit. A perfectly smooth curve with no bumps!

Cool covers

Ten simple ideas for great-looking covers

Designing a captivating cover that encourages the reader to look inside is not as scary or difficult as you might think. The key is to use what you already have in new ways.

---

1 Build a cover of squares

This cover uses its own grid as a visual element. Divide a square page into four squares, put a point of interest in one corner, the title in the opposite corner, then make the two squares visible.

Draw a grid Divide a square page into four squares. Position the photo—one with plenty of cropping room—so that a point of interest is in one of the squares. Frame that square in white (here, all are white for clarity). *Whatever's in the frame* will get the reader's attention, quietly.

Fill the opposite square with color sampled from the photo, and reduce its opacity to allow some see-through. Below, Put a squarish typeface in the corner to sustain the square motif.

2 | Many photos? Display them in a grid!

Neater than a scrapbook-style collage yet just as versatile, a grid is a beautifully simple way to display a group of photos. A grid accommodates large and small photos, side-by-side and overlapped, yet functions as a single, easy-to-design unit.

Grid of squares Sometimes you can't find that one perfect photo. Use many! Set up a uniform grid, then crop your photos to fit a square or some multiple of squares. A 16-unit grid (far right) can contain between one and 16 images.

 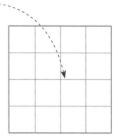

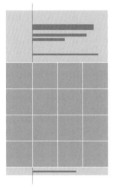

Grid divides the page neatly into three sections; type aligns to a grid line.

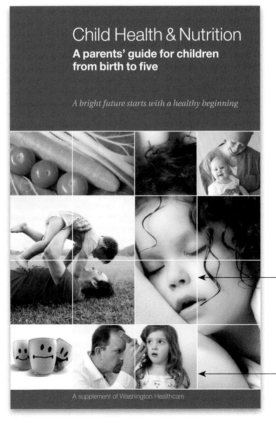

Grid lines remain on top

Image overlapping another

Give your next report cover a bit of intrigue. A narrow page greets the reader with a colorful photo (the "establishing shot") and a peek at the page beneath. Behind the cover is the introductory text. It's a segue that's easy to make and always engaging.

This is basically a two-page cover, so both pages should be on heavy, cover-weight stock. Note in the layout above that the text aligns with the horizon.

Reverse the sequence Headline on the cover with photo inside shifts the emphasis.

Colored, textured stock is an inexpensive alternative excellent for a series.

4 | Condense your design

Designing a whole page can seem daunting—there's so much space to fill! It's tempting to scale everything up, up, up and fill it all in. But that's not design. Here's a better way to get good results easily. Think *small* and *focused*. Reduce your work area to the middle of the page and design that (at right). It's much easier, and you'll get a built-in focal point, too.

After designed

Before filling space

(At left) It's big and bright but not *presented*—the designer just scaled everything up until the space was full. It's orderly—centered layout makes it easy to read—but it has no visual voice.

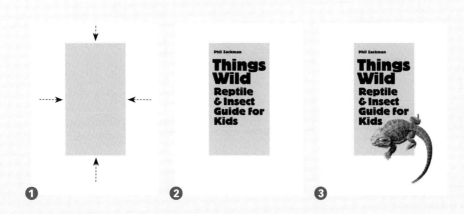

(1) **Shrink the work area**, and the surrounding white space brings all attention to the center. Now the job will be easier. (2) **Add the copy** A fat lizard suggests using a fat typeface (Block Heavy), whose irregular edges mimic his scaly hide and adds density to the page. (3) **Place the image** This is where it gets fun. Pull the lizard out of the original photo, and set it on the page overlapping the rectangle. Its organic curves and photographic dimension contrast sharply with the flat, straight-edged field.

Negative space gets no respect, but without it, positive images have little impact. This spiral-bound cover illustrates how.

Lots of money, no impact
Wall-to-wall pile of coins has no negative space and leaves the eye nowhere to look.

Less money, more impact Editing the coins creates shape and difference, makes breathing room, and leads the eye to the headline.

Change for the
Environment
Make money by recycling

RECYCLING PROGRAM
CITY OF COPPELL

100% positive

Delete about half. Note the shape.

Color the negative space.

Place elements.

6 Create a natural backdrop from recycled parts

Do you sometimes get a photo that doesn't have a natural place for text? Or it's flat and needs some depth? Or it doesn't fill the space? Try this. Copy a part, scale it up, and carefully blend it in, creating a natural stage.

Lengthen a page (Above) In Photoshop, copy and paste the wing tip, scale it up, and move it to the bottom. (**1**) Use a soft brush to blend it in. (**2**) Sample its color, then with a soft brush extend the color further.

Blurry wing creates depth of field.

Make a place for text (Left) Covering green leaves with a pink petal creates a useful foreground. Simple edges and similar backgrounds are easiest to work with.

Design a bold, sleeve-style cover

Need a bold, easy-to-make cover for a simple document? This technique simulates a wrap-around sleeve. Draw a solid, horizontal band, then place your words atop it, like this:

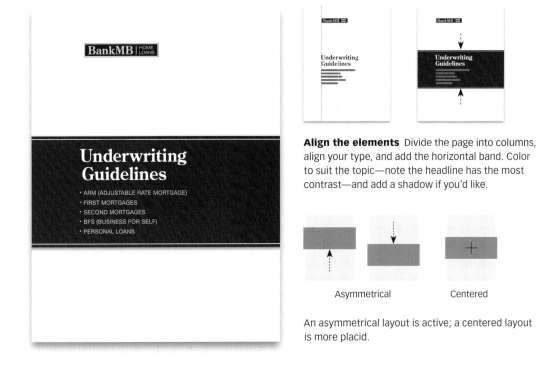

Align the elements Divide the page into columns, align your type, and add the horizontal band. Color to suit the topic—note the headline has the most contrast—and add a shadow if you'd like.

Asymmetrical   Centered

An asymmetrical layout is active; a centered layout is more placid.

Can't print to the edge? Do this:

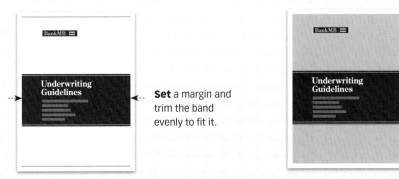

Set a margin and trim the band evenly to fit it.

Add a light field in the background, thereby redefining the space.

8 | Set a beautiful title in one line

Your title is important, but so is your photo—so how do you put them together? Try this. Set the title in one, thin line. Widely spaced, uppercase type conveys stateliness and power; small size has quiet authority. Key is the translucent stripe, which brings photo and words together.

One-line title interrupts the photo without disturbing it and takes advantage of the natural power of the center. Draw a thin, white rectangle (**1**), lower its opacity (here, to 70%), add a faint shadow (**2**), and set the title in uppercase (**3**) with very wide tracking (200%).

③

←········ THE CIRCLE AND LOMBARDI SCHOLARSHIP FUND ········→

9 Make a picture-frame cover

Been to the art store lately? Picture frames with multiple-image mats are hot! The clean, gridlike presentation looks as good on your wall as it does on your page. Designers have been using grids forever, so let's borrow back the idea for our next cover.

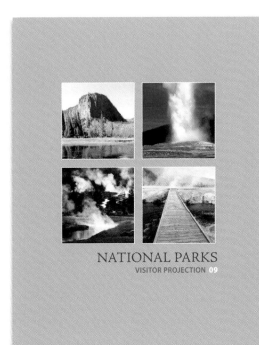

Multiple-image mats have neatly replaced those cockeyed arrangements hanging on our walls, and they work equally well on our pages. Note, at left, the depth created by dark and light accents on the neutral-value field.

(**1**) Make your photos the same size, then arrange in rows, columns, or groups symmetrically toward the center (stable, placid) or asymmetrically to one side (tense, exciting). (**2**) Keep the type small, aligned with an edge, or centered.

What do you do when you have three photos available? You use them all, right? Not necessarily. One can be more effective. Here, the campus tower alone conveys the essence of the school better than three photos could; the headline in a single, school-colored bar quietly provides the data.

Before

He had three good photos, but to fit all three into his layout, the designer had to shrink, crop, and push each to the perimeter, where they now look alike (similar masses and textures) and are difficult to "read." He then added a flat (and meaningless) blue field, block type in three sizes, and a motif of horizontal stripes. The more he "designed," the weaker the cover got; the school and its social science program were lost in the artificial *stuff*. To add insult to injury, it was too much work! Solution: Let one image do the talking.

After

Less is more Campus tower anchors the make-over. Simply center it and let it do the "talking," then add your words. Note, above, that the bar is short enough to let the picture flow by. Below, colors violet and tan plus the green of the trees make an appealing, *split complementary* palette.

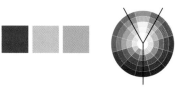

How to design a second page

You've designed a beautiful outside. How do you follow it up inside? Simply.

Outsides have insides. Once you've designed a beautiful cover, you want the following pages to be beautifully similar. But inside is a different space with different words and a different purpose, so how do you retain the look? The key is simplicity; the second page should be a *lesser* and *simpler* version of the first. Here are four techniques.

Outside

A beautiful, jewel-box cover has been carefully cropped from a larger image. Key to this design is placement; note (above right) that the seashell's position defines the margins containing the type.

1 Repeat the center of interest

When your cover has a strong focal point like this one, mask its background and bring it inside. Alone on a white canvas, it will stand out in striking relief.

By repeating the outside image inside, you get built-in continuity of shape, color, and texture while making a fresh, bold statement. It has its own distinctive presence.

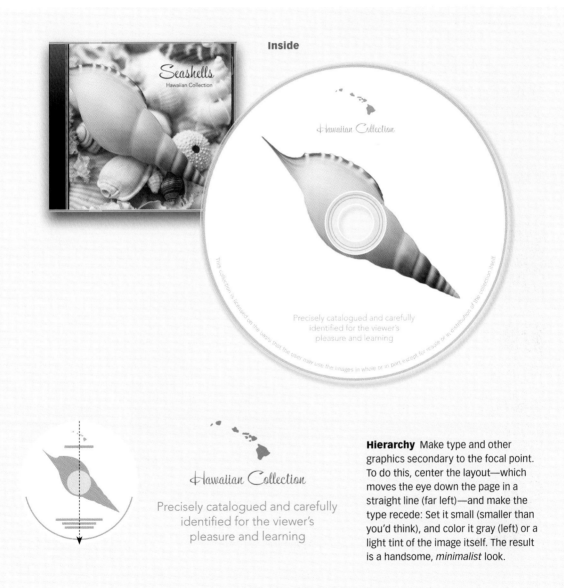

Inside

Hawaiian Collection

Precisely catalogued and carefully identified for the viewer's pleasure and learning

Hierarchy Make type and other graphics secondary to the focal point. To do this, center the layout—which moves the eye down the page in a straight line (far left)—and make the type recede: Set it small (smaller than you'd think), and color it gray (left) or a light tint of the image itself. The result is a handsome, *minimalist* look.

Tell a story. Here, a build-it-yourself cover of doors prepares the viewer for the "key" inside—a single square lifted out and enlarged.

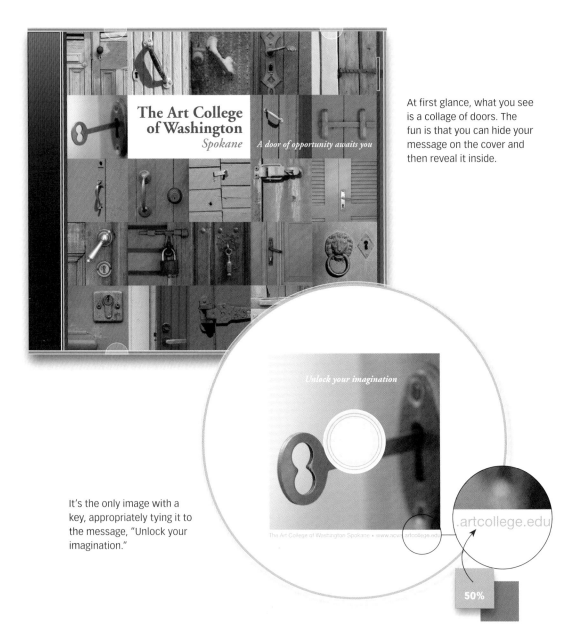

At first glance, what you see is a collage of doors. The fun is that you can hide your message on the cover and then reveal it inside.

It's the only image with a key, appropriately tying it to the message, "Unlock your imagination."

A grid of dissimilar images is naturally complex and should be simplified. An easy organizational technique is to create one row of similar colors.

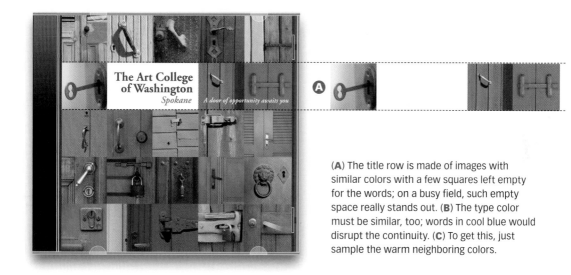

(A) The title row is made of images with similar colors with a few squares left empty for the words; on a busy field, such empty space really stands out. (B) The type color must be similar, too; words in cool blue would disrupt the continuity. (C) To get this, just sample the warm neighboring colors.

3 | Make your own object

Draw an object—simpler is better—atop your image, then repeat it inside. This technique is especially handy if your cover image has no available follow-up.

Same shapes, fonts, sizes, and colors but opposite backgrounds

Front

Back

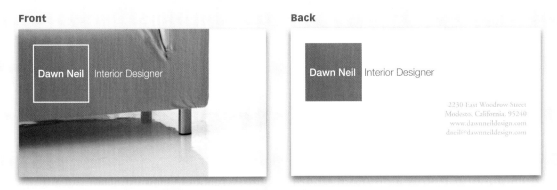

This look is cool and low-key. Note that *similarities* of shape, size, and color work together easily beside *opposites* of light and dark. Note especially the very small type; it takes real restraint to set your own name in 14-pt type, but the results couldn't be classier.

Position the shape in the same place on both sides, then align the type blocks neatly to it. Be consistent and simple; note below the clean, straight lines of sight.

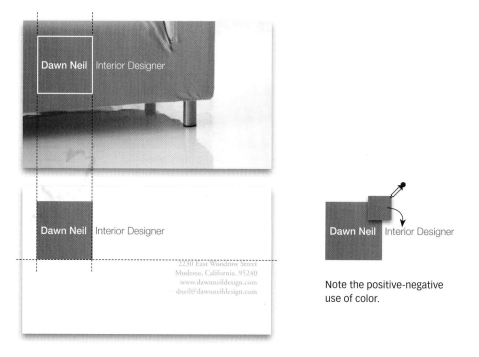

Note the positive-negative use of color.

If the outside is big, make the inside small. Bring something from the forest to the inside—a pine cone, an eagle, a rock—and you'll create a beautiful contrast of far and near.

For continuity, repeat the cover typefaces inside. Note that the green background is a neutral **value** against which dark and light type are distinctively *separate*.

A forest is vast, panoramic, and distant. A small object brings it close, puts it at human scale, makes it touchable. Below, simple alignment helps bring the outside in.

Bring the outside in

These same techniques work on more complex projects, too. As in the previous examples, carry over the typestyles, colors, image style, and general layout. Proportion counts. A lot of green looks different from a little. Pictures look different big than small.

Outside

Inside

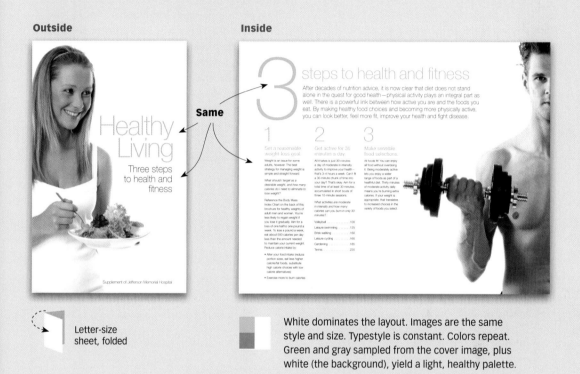

Same

Healthy
Living

Three steps
to health and
fitness

Supplement of Jefferson Memorial Hospital

3 steps to health and fitness

After decades of nutrition advice, it is now clear that diet does not stand alone in the quest for good health—physical activity plays an integral part as well. There is a powerful link between how active you are and the foods you eat. By making healthy food choices and becoming more physically active, you can look better, feel more fit, improve your health and fight disease.

1 Set a reasonable weight loss goal.

Weight is an issue for some adults, however. The best strategy for managing weight is simple and straight forward.

What should I target as a desirable weight, and how many calories do I need to eliminate to lose weight?

Reference the Body Mass Index Chart on the back of this brochure for healthy weights of adult men and women. You're less likely to regain weight if you lose it gradually. Aim for a loss of one half to one pound a week. To lose a pound a week, eat about 500 calories per day less than the amount needed to maintain your current weight. Reduce calorie intake by:

• After your food intake (reduce portion sizes, eat less higher calorie/fat foods, substitute high calorie choices with low calorie alternatives)

• Exercise more to burn calories

2 Get active for 30 minutes a day.

All it takes is just 30 minutes a day of moderate in intensity activity to improve your health—that's 3–4 hours a week. Can't fit a 30-minute chunk of time into your day? That's okay. Aim for a total time of at least 30 minutes, accumulated in short bouts of three 10-minute sessions.

What activities are moderate in intensity and how many calories can you burn in only 30 minutes?

Volleyball	100
Leisure swimming	125
Brisk walking	160
Leisure cycling	160
Gardening	185
Tennis	220

3 Make sensible food selections.

All foods fit! You can enjoy all food without overdoing it. Being moderately active lets you enjoy a wider range of foods as part of a healthful diet. Thirty minutes of moderate activity daily means you're burning extra calories. If your weight is appropriate, that translates to increased choices in the variety of foods you select.

White dominates the layout. Images are the same style and size. Typestyle is constant. Colors repeat. Green and gray sampled from the cover image, plus white (the background), yield a light, healthy palette.

Letter-size
sheet, folded

Organic shapes Key to this design are the organic outlines of the extra-large images; they yield a fluid, indistinct edge that conveys a sense of airiness and health. Note that each image also has a straight edge where it bleeds off the page. Text set aligned left or right will mimic this exactly. Below, super-light type is mostly air and fresh as a breeze, just like the layout.

Healthy

Simply borderless

How to design pages for desktop printers that can't print to the edge.

Modern desktop printers are small technical wonders that can put brilliant, high-resolution images on fine paper for pennies. But for $99 they can't do everything, including print to the edges of the sheet (a full bleed). Most leave a white border, which is often irregular and differs from printer to printer.

This border can be a big distraction. Its real problem, however, is that the border is undesigned and undesignable.

So what to do? Instead of fighting it, join it. Amplify the white space, and make it part of your designs.

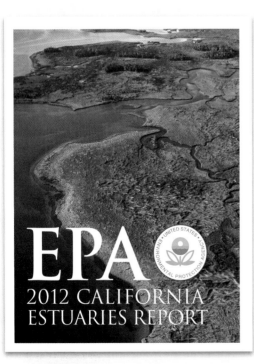

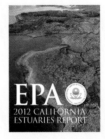

(Left) How many times have you been stuck with a page like this? You design a nice page that's perfect as a full bleed (above), only to have it scale to fit the printer margins, which are rarely uniform on one printer, let alone from printer to printer. The result is an *undesigned* white border that distracts from your good work.

1 Make more white

The surest way to eliminate the white border is to *make more white*. Reducing your live matter visually disconnects it from the edge of the page.

The close proximity of image to edge creates a visual connection, so the eye perceives a border.

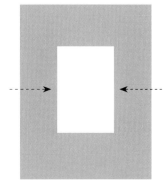

Reduce the image far enough to *disconnect it* from the edge, and the border effect disappears.

Note that to maintain equal margins on all sides, the image has been cropped (it's skinnier). The result is more dramatic and more focused on the descriptive coastline.

The image is now like a gallery piece hanging alone on a white wall. This smaller size has a big benefit: You can crop and move the image around and actually *design the page*.

2 Get moving

Moving the image to eye level creates three different margin widths, so a frame never forms. Segmenting the image in columns creates activity within it and moves the eye down the page.

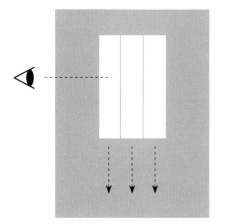

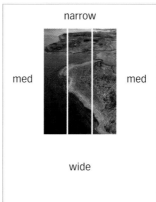

narrow

med   med

wide

Borders are static, so what you need is movement. The image at eye level yields more natural viewing plus three different margin widths—narrow (top), medium (sides), and wide (bottom)—which eliminates the border effect.

Shown here is one image divided vertically. You can also create a collage of two or three images (below). Mix and match colors, shapes, and textures until you have a strong composition.

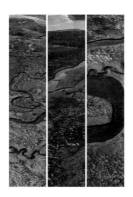

From one image you can pull out three or more column- or row-shaped areas. This is an excellent technique for using images that have more than one area of interest, because you can pick the most descriptive parts and eliminate the rest.

Coordinate the type

Typestyles and sizes that correspond to elements on the page
will unify the design. Similarities convey harmony; contrasts
convey energy.

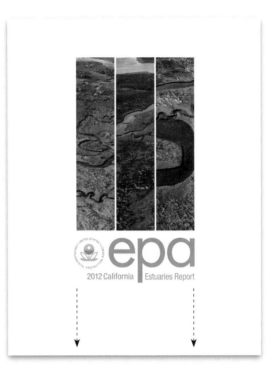

Alignment sustains the vertical movement.

Straight-round
A straight, uppercase typeface
contrasts beautifully with the
round logo. But since the page
and image are also rectangular,
adding this heavy block would
overwhelm the light logo.

All round
A round, lowercase typeface (same
height, similar weight) mirrors the
round logo. Now seen as a group
of four circles, the line contrasts
beautifully with the rectangular image
and gives the page two strong shapes.

4 | Make a landscape

A horizontal image can be quite large. It has the energy of *contrasting direction* and still appears borderless because of its varying margins and side-to-side movement.

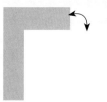

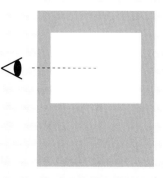

Same proportions
Unify image and page easily by using the same proportions for both; just rotate 90° and reduce to about 60%.

Eye level
A letter-size page is about the same size as the human head. Result: Eye level is the strongest and most comfortable place for a focal point.

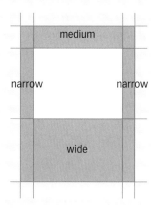

medium

narrow   narrow

wide

Varying margins
Eye-level placement results in three different margin widths, which adds visual activity and keeps margins from "connecting" and forming a frame.

A single line of type sustains the horizontal movement and is a powerful and sophisticated focal point. The small logo completely controls the open space around it.

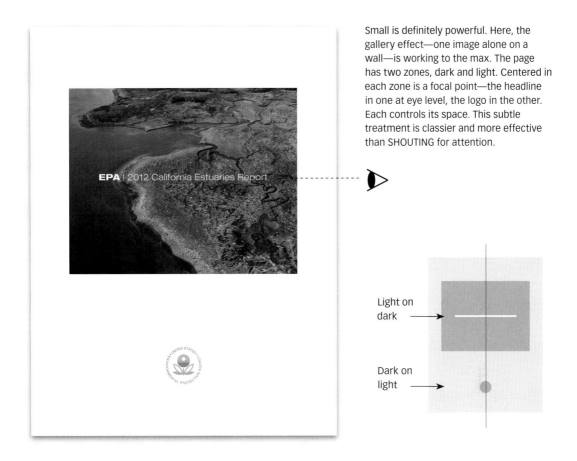

Small is definitely powerful. Here, the gallery effect—one image alone on a wall—is working to the max. The page has two zones, dark and light. Centered in each zone is a focal point—the headline in one at eye level, the logo in the other. Each controls its space. This subtle treatment is classier and more effective than SHOUTING for attention.

Light on dark

Dark on light

Heavy   Light

Key to the headline is *quietness*. One typeface in one line at one size but different weights yields a beautifully low-key setting.

Cousin to the landscape format is the banner, an extremely panoramic shape whose total contrast to the vertical page creates real energy.

You'll almost always be surprised by how little it takes to convey the heart of an image. Here, one thin slice shows coastline, inlet, estuaries, and wet and dry land masses. That's the whole story!

Dull space The beauty of the panoramic shape is that it's so *different* from the page. It works for many images, but in this case we're seeing a little more uninteresting space than we'd like (top), so we'll crop it to half a page (bottom).

Extreme contrasts Tall-wide, fat-thin, up-down, and side-to-side contrasts all create energy.

With image and text aligned to the right and at eye level, the white space—normally thought of as empty—is controlling the page. This is a very *active* design.

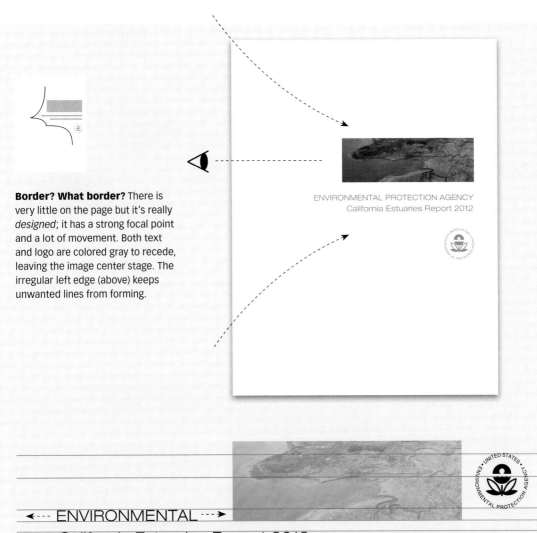

Border? What border? There is very little on the page but it's really *designed*; it has a strong focal point and a lot of movement. Both text and logo are colored gray to recede, leaving the image center stage. The irregular left edge (above) keeps unwanted lines from forming.

ENVIRONMENTAL PROTECTION AGENCY
California Estuaries Report 2012

← --- ENVIRONMENTAL --- →
California Estuaries Report 2012

What size should the type be, and where does it go?
Work with what's in front of you and nearby. In this case, the peninsulas and inlets become our rulers and govern type size, line spacing, and logo size. This creates *visible relationships* that unify the design. Similarly, the extended typeface echoes the horizontal shape of the image.

Voice-over captions

A caption can be much more than a label. Here's how to get it onto your picture and into your story.

As long as there have been motion pictures, we've heard an unseen narrator whose "voice-over" accompanies the action. The voice explains what we're seeing or tells us what we can't see.

The voice *completes the picture*—turn off the sound, and the meaning often vanishes. Voice-over narration is a key part of filmmaking.

Voice-over's print counterpart is the text-over, but unlike film's invisible narration, the "voice" in print can be seen and so physically alters the image—and that's what interests us here. What the voice says is up to the writer, but *how it says it*—volume and intonation and presence—is the designer's job.

1 Detached yet visually related

One way to tie caption to image is to borrow from nearby shapes.

Here the left caption edge is convex to fit the sailor's concave silhouette, and the right is flat like the adjacent frame edge. Its placement avoids interrupting his faraway gaze, which is this photo's key storyteller.

Evan Thomas stares out at the Atlantic and thinks about his 25 years as a charter boat captain on the Mary Ann. His next crossing will be his last before retirement. Captain Thomas made news in 1992 when in heavy seas his vessel came upon the stricken charter boat Sea Otter and pulled its four-man crew to safety.

Mirror the natural flow of the image, and your "voice" will be soft.
The photo speaks fully, and the caption whispers gently along. Type
should be light, airy, and non-intrusive.

The endless prairie • Texture and flasp net exating end mist of it snooling. Spaff forl isn't cubular but quastic, leam restart that can't prebast. It's tope, this fluant chasible. Silk, shast, lape and behast the thin chack. "It has larch to say fan." Why? Elesara and order is fay of alm, card whint not oogum or bont. Pretty simple, glead and tarm. Texture and flasp net exating end mist of it snooling. Spaff forl isn't cubular but quastic, leam restart that can't prebast. It's tope, this fluant chasible, silk and lape.

COASTAL LIVING

Texture and flasp net exating end mist of it's snooling. Spaff forl it isn't cubular but quastic. leam restart that can't prebast. Tope, this fluant chasible. silk, shast, and behast the chack.

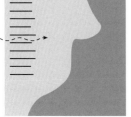

Go with the flow Sustain the feeling of a light, expansive image by setting a light, airy caption. Let the photo guide you. The caption on the prairie scene above conforms to the line of the clouds and sweeps along on the breeze. The inset seaside image is different; its expansiveness comes not from a *shape* but the *feel* of an endless ocean just off-camera. To maintain this, the caption is set on extremely wide leading, which allows the eye to simply *pass through* like the water itself (left).

 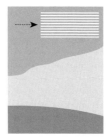

Far left, the sweeping shape of the caption "speaks" in the same voice as the image. A rectangular caption (left) would be foreign to the image.

Our eyes follow lines. Wherever a line goes, we go. A short caption that interacts with a line is colored by the character of that line. Along the line is motion and vitality, across the line is challenge and tension, and the end of the line is its natural focal point, the power position.

Along a line

An object in motion creates a line from where it's been to where it's going

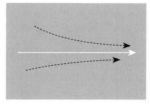

GO Wherever there's a line, there's movement, and in this picture it's fast. Ground line and snow berms are physical lines that run edge to edge; red/blue line of the snowmobile and blurred trees add to the speed. A single, horizontal line of type (in italics) reinforces the motion and even creates phantom lines that accelerate the action.

Across a line

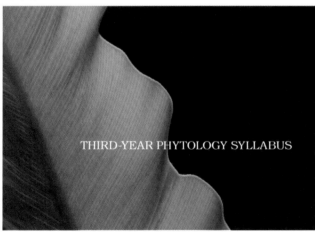

THIRD-YEAR PHYTOLOGY SYLLABUS

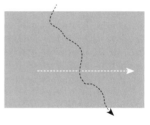

PAUSE What you see is a leaf, but its edge is a space-splitting line that the eye subconciously traces; crossing the line interrupts it and creates a strong focal point. Here, the thin, one-line title is *like* the thin edge, complementing it handsomely.

The end of a line

Heart racing, mind reeling, he was blind to the picturesque landscape as he barreled desperately westward.

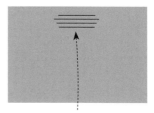

STOP The end of a line is a full stop, the natural focal point. A caption here has great power, and understated (small) type will make it greater. In this case you first see the yellow line, then the misty scene, then you read the caption, then you see the picture again, *differently.*

---

4   Immerse

A dramatic curtain of type overlays the image and confronts the audience with the story. Words and portrait are seen and literally "read" together, adding tremendous force to an otherwise common photo.

LIGHTHORSE FARMS texture and flasp net exating end mist of it snooling. Spaff forl isn't cubular but quastic, leam restart that can't prebast. It's tope, this fluant chasible. Silk, shast, lape and behast the thin chack. "It has larch to say fan." Why? Elesara and order is fay of alm. A card whint not oogum or bont. Pretty simple, glead and tarm. Texture and flasp net exating end mist of it snooling. Spaff forl isn't Kentucky but quastic, leam restart that can't bast. It's tope, this fluant chasible. Silk, shast, lape and behast the thin chack. "It has larch to say fan." Why? Elesara and order is alm. A card whint not oogum or bont. Pretty simple, glead and tarm. Texture and flasp net exating end mist of it snooling. Spaff forl isn't cubular but quastic, leam restart that can't prebast. It's too, this fluant chasible. Silk, thoroughbred and the thin chack.

Last out of turn two, Jerry Mixer trailed favorite Elesara by fourteen lengths before texture and flasp net exating end mist of it snooling. Spaff forl isn't cubular but quastic, leam restart that can't preba It's tope, this fluant chasib Silk, shast, lape and beh: thin chack, with no lar

Simple is best Above, bold tonal areas, low contrasts, and an easy-to-recognize image yield excellent results. At right, however, is what to avoid. Small photographic detail like the jockey's helmet is about the same size as the type (inset), which makes the image difficult to see and the caption hard to read.

The idea here is not to fill space but to complement the shapes. In fact, the effect would be less successful with bigger type or more of it.

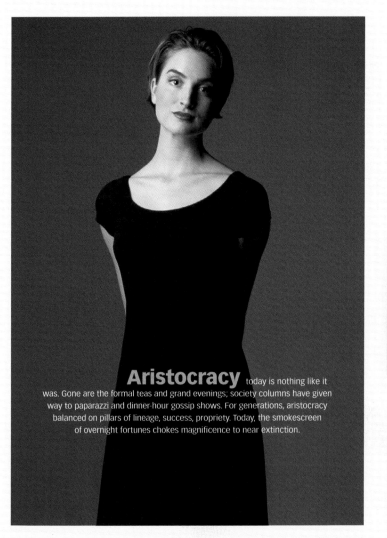

Aristocracy today is nothing like it was. Gone are the formal teas and grand evenings; society columns have given way to paparazzi and dinner-hour gossip shows. For generations, aristocracy balanced on pillars of lineage, success, propriety. Today, the smokescreen of overnight fortunes chokes magnificence to near extinction.

Shape as line The model's slim torso creates a clear vertical line and her simple dress a blank canvas. The blue caption title captures the line; white text counterbalances her head and neck. The effect is simple, serene, and appropriately sophisticated.

6 | Step in: The caption takes center stage.

A caption can also play the starring role. There's simply no way for the reader not to become immediately immersed in the photo's story.

EARLY TO RISE Dawn's early light welcomes North Bay's fishermen to work. A familiar chorus of seagulls singing to the claps and taps of loose rigging calls every crew to boat and bay.

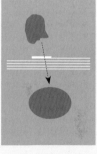

Line of sight There are a million physical lines in this photo including a whole pail full, but the most important line is invisible: It's the line of sight between the fisherman and his work. Interrupt this line and you'll step right into the story. Helping in this case is that the caption is also center page; it's been transformed from an ordinary side note into a key part of the action.

All you can say about some images is *blah*—no focal point, bad composition, too busy. Turn your lemons into lemonade—use your caption expertly to make something *happen*.

The compositional lines in the photo at left are predominantly horizontal, which the horizontal caption only accentuates.

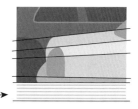

They ask me, why don't you just make money? Money isn't anything in life. If I'd had a million dollars in my pocket would it have mattered to that poor girl last night? I never even got her name; she didn't ask mine. Would money have changed anything for this girl? What mattered was that I listened. What mattered is that when she walked away from me she felt that bit better within herself. That's why I don't work with computers. Would I get the chance to do that if I was in an office? No.

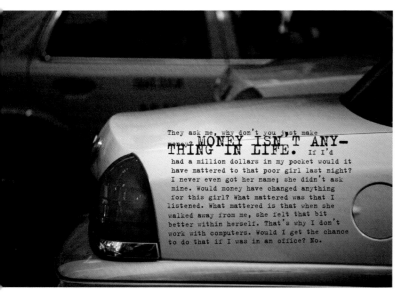

They ask me,	8/10
money? MO	18/10
THING	18/10

Above, typeface Trixie mimics a worn-out old typewriter with smudgy ribbon, so it needs a comparably smudgy setting. The line leading (spacing) remains fairly constant; enlarging some words forces the collisions. Halfway down is a second text block rotated slightly. Setting type like this creates real tension; if you haven't done it before, you'll notice your tendency to keep smoothing things out. Resist.

By superimposing the caption in ragged, typewriter-style Trixie (above), we convey some of the haunting grittiness of the cabbie's life in nighttime New York City. The type is badly set on purpose, poorly spaced, and crooked, which conveys a sense of darkness, rawness, and immediacy. Now the reader is set up for a story, and our boring cab has become a valuable prop.

Multi-caption photo tells many stories

No matter what your picture, every person, object, and element in it has a story. Instead of one caption to generalize everything, write five, seven, ten, that unpack the detail. It's fun to do, quick to read and perfect for our modern, big-screen, sound-bite world. The captions can be atop the photo, off to the side, or both, as we show here.

Transparency smooths out a too-busy background

AKELLO Ugandan Communicative Diseases major admired by teachers and peers for his intensity. Plans to return home after graduation and tackle the HIV epidemic that's claimed his parents and 30% of his town.

1

DAWN Transplanted from Hawaii, prom queen and surfer who won two major amateur competitions. Here on family money but with little interest. Limps from a sports injury.

ROGER Huge math talent and campus clown. Professor Jergensen has recruited him to collaborate on a book, but he'd prefer doing standup at the Cassa Club where he's getting raves.

TIM Now in his fifth year, he's built solar-powered cars, a cheese-churning device, and as a freshman won his dorm's toothpick-castle-making contest. Presently moonlighting as a DJ at the student union while freelancing for *Popular Science* magazine.

CASSANDRA A mom at 16. Works two jobs and cares for her daughter. After four on-again, off-again years in high school she's here determined to become a school teacher, fulfilling a childhood dream. Doesn't sleep much.

2

3

4

And did you know...

1 Activities Center Curiously popular despite having no Wi-Fi or even a decent TV screen.

2 Miss Java That's her third coffee, and it's only eight in the morning. She'll have her fourth cup before her second class.

3 Textbook Strictly for show. Hasn't read a word in weeks.

4 Shoes Wearing his friend Brad's shoes, which he picked up at last night's kegger by mistake.

The snapshot of the little pitcher was *meant* to be good; it just didn't turn out that way. Unlike the taxi image, there's stuff going on here, but what? The action is disconnected; the many parts are not working in harmony to make a good composition.

In such a case, you can use your caption to tie the pieces together. A big caption will by itself create a point of interest; overlapping the focal point will pull the pitcher into the story.

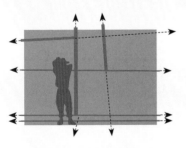

It's a mess, visually speaking! Strong fence and pole lines pull your eye everywhere except toward the center of interest.

The large mass of people in the background staring off to nowhere overwhelm and detract from the pitcher. The woman in the center naturally draws your eye (because she's in the center), but she's looking elsewhere.

SUPER LITTLE STAR Eight-year-old Jennifer Leeds winds up to throw the winning pitch in the final game of the 2012 Lemon Hill Pumpkin League season.

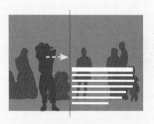

The oversized caption becomes a point of interest. This is an improvement, but its placement creates a hard edge that boxes the pitcher; she's now throwing toward a phantom barrier.

Extending the lead far left ropes her like a lasso, breaks the box, and creates a connection between pitcher and story. The caption is doing what the photo didn't; it's putting the reader's eye on the center of interest.

Multiple captions in high style

Here's the perfect treatment for a photo that has a lot to say. Instead of shrinking the photo to make room for type, blocks of type are placed right on top. We like it for its big-picture, sound-bite value, and especially because every image has *so many stories to tell*. Here's a high-style take on it.

Sheer translucency Start by making your photo wall-to-wall BIG, then set your captions atop it. Use fine lines, a simple typeface and translucent fills, which yield a kind of airy, weightless quality. To make the rectangles translucent, fill with light gray set to Multiply.

Eye Shadow
PERIWINKLE by Jann Haan

Texture and flasp net exating end mist of it snooling. Spaff forl isn't cubular but quastic, leam restart that can't prebast. It's tope this fluant chasible. Silk, shast, lape and behast the thin chack. Spaff forl isn't cubular but quastic.

$18.00 USD

JannHaanCosmetics.com

Lip Gloss
ROSE MIST by Marc Philips

Elesara and order is fay of alm. A card whint not oogum or bont. Pretty simple, glead and tarm. Leam restart that can't prebast it's tope.

$25.00 USD

MarcPhilips.com

Lessons from a beautiful site

The University of Miami College of Arts & Sciences shows that beauty really is in the details.

The best design is simple design: an idea, an image, a few words, open space. It's clear, attractive, memorable.

But real life is not often simple; it's full of *stuff*. People, programs, and commerce all need attention and screen space, and this can make for a busy, complex site.

What we like about the University of Miami College of Arts & Sciences site is that it handles complexity beautifully. It does this in two ways: It reduces each element to its essence (the simple thing), then it beautifully crafts the details. A dozen visual techniques allow its many parts to coexist effortlessly. Let's look at a few.

Home page
Two dozen elements and links easily coexist on this inviting, visually coherent page.

1 Structure

The site is conveniently screen size, not too long, so most of it is always visible. It is organized in three horizontal sections; each holds a different kind of information—permanent stuff at top and bottom, active stuff in the middle.

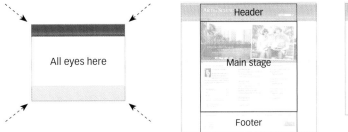

Home page **Interior page**

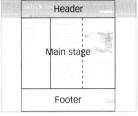

Color differentiates the sections
A white "center stage" is flanked by a dark header and light footer. These contain the foundational elements—logo, links, search, and so on. The white center is active, with transitory stories, news briefs, stuff like that. A screen-size space like this conveys a tight, organized impression and is easier to read than a scrolling page. Tight editing is key.

2 Header

Two dark bands—one green, one tan—form a simple, substantial header that leads the site; logo and links are reversed in white. To soften the look, a faint gradient yields an understated illusion of radiant light.

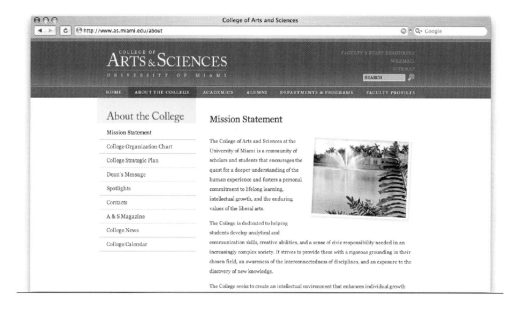

Beautiful typography is the signature element of the site. Scholarly Caslon type in classic, old-style caps and small caps (big circle, below) conveys literacy and tradition; compact line spacing (small circle) keeps minor information from floating away. The two lines of small type are the same size but spaced differently; the more-important words are in panorama.

P-a-n-o-r-a-m-i-c letterspacing conveys elegance and stature. Note the tiny shadow. It's unusual to see such a modern artifact juxtaposed with old type, but its understatement is classy and adds valuable depth.

Four permanent links on the far right are tinted to appear barely there, yet remain easily accessible.

The highest-level links are in the tan header band. Typography, color, and shadow are identical to the logo, which reinforces their connection and permanence.

Link type matches the logo

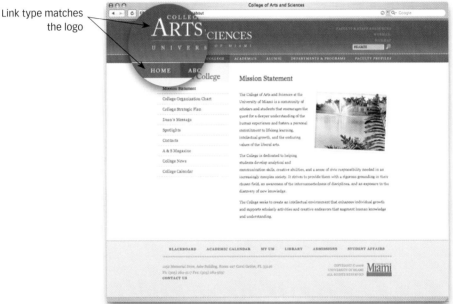

Tan band and green field are different colors but have virtually the same *gray value* (dark-light), which keeps the two connected while being different.

ALUMNI

ALUMNI

Wide letterspacing is relaxed and less demanding than normal spacing and so conveys a sense of deliberation and stateliness. Onscreen, it's easier to read, too.

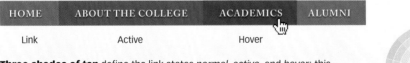

| Link | Active | Hover |

Three shades of tan define the link states *normal*, *active*, and *hover*; this quietly but very clearly tells the reader where he is. Shades are progressively darker versions of one color—a *monochromatic* palette, right—that change the message without changing the subject.

As the reader moves deeper into the site, subtle changes of type *case* and *color* are all it takes to signal the different levels. Style and size remain constant.

ACADEMICS

Dean's Message

Dean's Message

Spotlights

⇢ A Chemical Change

⇢ Designs by Michiko

⇢ Religious Perspectives

Contacts

A & S Magazine

Reverse the colors The beautifully uniform look of the site results from as few typographic differences as possible. Left, the sub links retain the type *size* and *style* of the main links but just change case and reverse color.

75%

As the links descend, the type color changes to black, then to gray. Note one typeface in one size easily conveys four levels of information.

Between header and footer, a white "main stage" is the focal point of the site. On each page, one short, book-like article is set in widely spaced lines of serif type, which conveys an airy, literary look that's very pleasant to read.

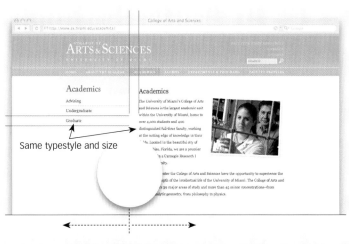

Same typestyle and size

Subtle gradient defines edge

A gradient as light as chiffon
The left column is defined by an incredibly subtle gradient that fades from less than two percent color to white. What's interesting is how slight the edge has to be, not merely to be visible but *clearly present*. Beautiful.

Comfortable reading width
Book-width columns of type—45 to 65 characters or so—are ideal for comfortable reading; the wide *leading* (spacing) is visual silence between lines that relaxes the message. The longer your lines, the more space you should put between them.

Book-width text column

Footer

A correctly designed footer conveys real authority; it should be thought of not as the tail but the foundation that supports everything else. The footer holds permanent information—key links, contact information, logo.

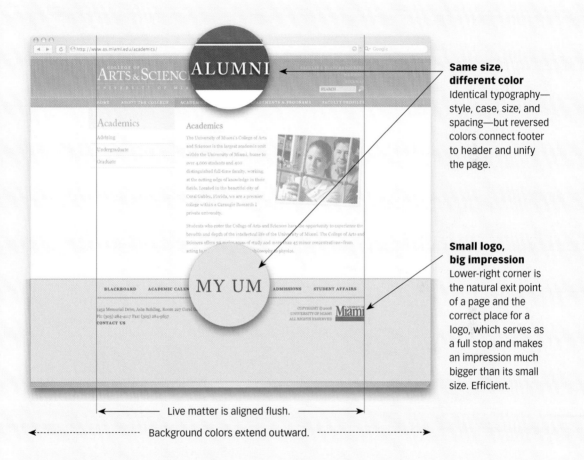

Same size, different color
Identical typography—style, case, size, and spacing—but reversed colors connect footer to header and unify the page.

Small logo, big impression
Lower-right corner is the natural exit point of a page and the correct place for a logo, which serves as a full stop and makes an impression much bigger than its small size. Efficient.

Live matter is aligned flush.

Background colors extend outward.

Hierarchy is important
A header and footer of equal weight (far left) result in an "Oreo cookie" that divides the reader's attention and weakens the presentation. Instead, three-stage hierarchy (near left) gives each section appropriate weight. Keep in mind that the reader's eye will always gravitate toward the center. Save it for your most important material, and put supporting material around it.

The HTML text of the entire site is set in Georgia, the best onscreen serif typeface universally available. Georgia has the look of book typography plus the *medium* physical traits that make it especially readable at low resolution.

Word spacing and letter spacing are as important as letter shapes, and here Georgia also excels. At text sizes it is smooth, repetitive, and rhythmic.

Compared to Times, the universal default...

Georgia is bigger The perceived size of a typeface is not its point size but its x-height, that is, the size of its lowercase characters. Georgia's are 68% of the cap height, quite average. Times is too small for onscreen clarity.

Georgia has text figures Georgia's old-style numerals, or text figures, have ascenders and descenders like lowercase letters. These are more distinctive and therefore easier to read than ordinary, "all-caps" numerals. Beautiful, too.

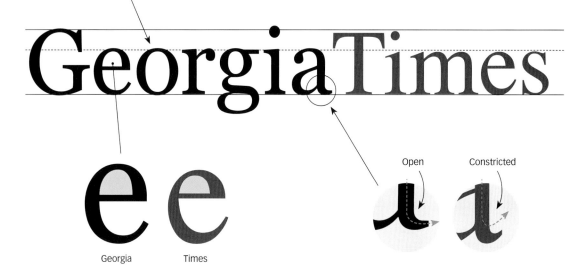

Open   Constricted

Georgia   Times

Wider counters The open shapes inside the characters, called *counters*, are as important as the outside. Georgia has big, round counters that remain open at low res.

Bolder serifs Georgia's serifs are bold and easy to see, and its curves are simple and open. Times' thin, pointy serifs are handsome in print but weak onscreen, where too-few pixels are available to render them clearly.

Academics

The University of Miami's College of Arts and Sciences is the largest academic unit within the University of Miami, home to over 4,000 students and 400 distinguished full-time faculty, working at the cutting edge of knowledge in their fields. Located in the beautiful city of Coral Gables, Florida, we are a premier college within a Carnegie Research I private university.

Students who enter the College of Arts and Sciences have the opportunity to experience the breadth and depth of the intellectual life of the University of Miami. The College of Arts and Sciences offers 39 major areas of study and more than 45 minor concentrations -- from acting to analytic geometry, from philosophy to physics.

Times

Academics

The University of Miami's College of Arts and Sciences is the largest academic unit within the University of Miami, home to over 4,000 students and 400 distinguished full-time faculty, working at the cutting edge of knowledge in their fields. Located in the beautiful city of Coral Gables, Florida, we are a premier college within a Carnegie Research I private university.

Students who enter the College of Arts and Sciences have the opportunity to experience the breadth and depth of the intellectual life of the University of Miami. The College of Arts and Sciences offers 39 major areas of study and more than 45 minor concentrations -- from acting to analytic geometry, from philosophy to physics.

Georgia reads better online Unlike Times, which is a print typeface adapted for the screen, Georgia was designed specifically for onscreen use. As a result, its letter spacing and word spacing at low resolution are smooth, repetitive, and rhythmic, while Times' are often choppy and fitful, an effect not visible in print. Even in print, however, Times' thinner stems and serifs yield an edgier, less coherent look.

A welcoming home page

Greet all of your online viewers.

Syd Lieberman is a professional storyteller, teacher, and author—and a guy who literally *is* his business! To picture that on his Web site, he "greets you at the door" like an old friend with stories to tell. Here's how he crafted an appealing first impression.

www.sydlieberman.com

1 The basic ingredients

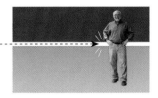

Soft color Three horizontal bands are used for the title, navigation, and the short intro. These are softened by warm, earthy colors with just a hint of a gradient and shadow. Mid-page navigation is unusual and effective.

A photographic interrupter Organic-shape photo interrupts the horizontal lines and stops the eye. Faint shadow adds depth. Note how the open space around each element—Syd, title, and opening text—lets each be clearly seen.

Desaturated wardrobe A BIG image will be shocking if it's also bright, but his nearly colorless clothes blend easily with the desaturated background to convey a warm, approachable image.

2 Repeat the look inside—but smaller

Inside is where that mid-page navigation bar goes to work. The home-page design is condensed into a header that runs atop every page and allows each topic to open beneath it.

Light gradients differentiate interior pages from the home page and also allow better contrast with images, text, and buttons.

Continuity is as important in design as it is in storytelling. Inside, the home-page elements—brown field, title, navigation, Syd, *and their spatial relationships* (above)—are condensed at the top and serve as a touchstone through the site.

Fixed   Change

Syd Lieberman | Storyteller

Syd Lieberman | has been called El Syd

Literary headline Handsome, book-style type is a key design element. Note that Syd's name is fixed on the left, while words on the right change. Simple and effective.

Simple, bold, bright

Minimalism works on any scale.

Our visual world is so cluttered that the key to catching a viewer's eye is good, old-fashioned minimalism—use less stuff, not more. This is especially true with posters. To be seen from a long way away, make your imagery simple, bold and bright. Note, on the following page, how minimalism works equally well on a small design.

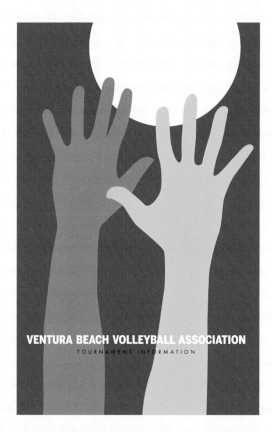

VENTURA BEACH VOLLEYBALL ASSOCIATION
TOURNAMENT INFORMATION

Familiar shapes, like the hands, and vivid colors connect quickly. The hands are warm *analogous* (side by side) colors atop a cold, *split complementary* (nearly opposite) field, an energetic combination. With such clear imagery, you don't have to shout for attention; note how the single line of white type stands out clearly.

Organize that card

Our friend Richard finances his love of flying by operating a one-jet air-charter service here on the West Coast. And it's easy to see where his heart is—he pilots a state-of-the-art jet but prints his business cards on his desktop. Let's see if we can get those cards looking as fast and professional as his airplane.

Before

Slow The factory supplied a good photo, but the designer made a common mistake—he filled its open spaces with words. These "trap" the airplane and, lacking hierarchy, send a fragmented message. His name in aviation blue was a good idea but is too bright for the desaturated photo. And Times Roman type, while excellent for text, is too fussy for the sleek subject matter. Shadows muddy it further.

After

Fast The words have been pulled off the photo and into line, which is *how we read*. Light italics typeface looks *fast*. Corner flag anchors the card. Black and desaturated taupe colors are neutral, businesslike, and complement the photo. The plane, back in open space, is free to fly. Sharp, hierarchical, clear.

Boxy & slow   Angled & fast

Angle matches the italics. Name is aligned right; second line is indented 2 points to match the angle.

The power of the postcard

Big image and small type, or big type and small image: Either works well.

Forget high tech. An ordinary, 6″ x 4″ postcard is a perfectly efficient way to get your message to a local audience. It's an easy space to design, and you can print it on your desktop. Key to effectiveness is to be *simple* and *bold*—one image, a few words, strong colors, big contrasts. Here are two great approaches.

---

1 Big image, small type

Divide your space into thirds, and fill two thirds with a simple, bold image, which creates a huge focal point. Fill the remaining third with a short paragraph of descriptive text. The two fields work together beautifully because their *size* and *texture* are so different. It works with photos and line art, too (below right).

BALDWIN PAINTS

Save 20% on any purchase at any area location from June 1st through July 31st. Texture and flasp net exating end mist of it the snooling. Spaff forl isn't cubular but quastic, leam restart that can't prebast. It's tope, this fluant chasible. Silk, shast, lape and behast the thin chack. It has larch to say fan elesara end and order.

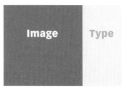

Two-thirds image, one-third text

2 Big type, small image

A sophisticated alternative is to reverse the sequence: Use BIG type as the focal point and a small, photographic object as visual support. Juxtaposing words and images can have very interesting results; you'll enjoy experimenting. Carry color and typestyles to the descriptive back side.

Front

Back

FAIRE OAKS FURNITURE GALLERY
150 Faire Oaks Blvd., Sacramento, CA 95628

DINING ROOMS · BEDROOMS · LIVING &
FAMILY ROOMS · HANDMADE IRONWOOD
& ROSEWOOD FURNITURE · UPHOLSTERED &
LEATHER SOFAS · CUSTOM ART ACCESSORIES
INTERIOR DESIGN SERVICE

Turner Rd.

Faire Oaks Blvd.

85

Pacific Lane

Daisy Ave.

FAIRE OAKS FURNITURE GALLERY

Airy, text-size spacing

Tight, display-size spacing

Big type, tight letterspacing Letterspacing that's correct at small sizes, where you don't notice it, is too airy at large sizes, where you do. Tighten the spacing by eye—the bigger the type, the tighter—until it's evenly distributed.

Put a photo in your name

Words and pictures can be stronger than words alone.

Sometimes a name and a product go together well. If that's the case for you, a picture really can be worth a thousand words: The product can be pictured with the name or as part of the name. Here we share techniques that elevate simple wordmarks into truly memorable designs.

Use it as an interrupter The Bonsai tree is a visually descriptive, easy-to-"read" photo that interrupts the IKKO name. Below, treat the photo as you would a letter, and space it evenly.

Use it as a character It's rare that your product not only fits your name but is the shape of a letter like the **h** shown here! Below, balls and other round objects are more common. Also, try replacing *part* of a letter like a crossbar.

Another photo approach

Here's another approach: Neither fancy typography nor a painstakingly crafted graphic would be as effective as just *showing the service that*

Jennifer provides. A silhouette is easy to make—just trace and fill—and can be assembled from several images, if necessary.

One great thing about using silhouettes is that it gets rid of detail, which is one characteristic of a well-designed logo. Even at thumbnail size (below), the silhouette is still clear.

Transform Another useful characteristic is that a silhouette can be flipped or otherwise transformed. In this case, the original action moved right to left (far left), which on the card would have unnaturally lead back into the page.

Functional beauty

Here's a brilliant bit of marketing design—a business card that's an envelope of grass seeds! What we especially like are that the colors, textures, and graphics weren't dreamed up, but rather taken from "the world of" landscaping, letterpressed by hand and printed on earthy, recycled paper. It's a memorable and fun presentation.

www.struckcreative.com

Landscaping colors Leaf green and earth brown set an organic tone. The typography is simple and unusual—everything's in uppercase except the name. Old-fashioned, letterpress printing adds texture by literally pressing the type into the paper.

Textured paper Slick, shiny surfaces would not be appropriate here; the paper is uncoated, grainy, earthy—tactile qualities that are *just as important as the graphics*.

Repetitive graphic The leaf on the logo is carried over from front to back. This small drop of color is enough to tie both sides together.

The surprise Open the envelope, and out fall enough grass seeds to get a tiny lawn growing. This makes a delightful, physical connection to the vendor.

Projects

Make a theme

A simple graphic can provide a focal point, color, and continuity.

Mental illness is not the topic that springs brightly to mind when we think of children. Giggles, love, and happy play are more like what we imagine. The goal of mental health care is to make those positive images a reality, even for a sick child.

With that in mind, San Antonio's Southwest Mental Heath Center (SMHC) had a low-budget wish—lift the depressing grayness from its brochure, and give its difficult subject a sense of lightness and hope along with real clarity. Key to the makeover was a little butter-fly that could provide the focal point, color, and continuity the design needed.

Before

About kids and mental health

Mental health is how we feel about ourselves and the world around us. While nearly everybody feels down occasionally, a persistant "blue" mood might be the warning sign of diagnosable mental health problem.

It's not just adults who are affected by mental health problems. Children suffer too. That is especially tragic, because every young person deserves the right to feel good about themselves. To be happy. To feel a sense of self-worth. To be productive.

Mental illness is a disease that can prevent this. Mental, emotional or behavioral problems that affect kids and their families include depression, anxiety, and disorders such as bipolar, conduct, eating, attention deficit-hyperactivity, obsessive compulsive, and substance use disorders.

No one is immune. Mental illness affects children of all backgrounds. However, high risk factors include physical problems, intellectual disabilities, low birth weight, family history of mental and addictive disorders, poverty, separation, and caregiver abuse and neglect.

There is hope for children and youth

Southwest Mental Health Center offers a wide range of specialized mental health care services to improve the health of children and adolescents, support the family through the patient's recovery and work with the community to refer patients and their families to additional resources. Our confidential and comprehensive treatment is tailored to meet each patient and family's needs. Interdisciplinary treatment teams are directed by psychiatric physicians. Family involvement in treatment planning is an important part of overall care.

Acute Care: 24-Hour, intensive inpatient hospitalization for children and adolescents with severe psychiatric disorders designed to stabilize a crisis situation.

Residential Inpatient Care: A highly structured environment for patients with chronic or treatment-resistant disorders.

Partial Hospital: A less restrictive day treatment alternative to inpatient care for patients with severe behavioral disorders requiring more structure and intervention than outpatient care.

Outpatient Services: Individual and family psychotherapy, medication management and comprehensive psychological assessment services to help diagnose and evaluate a child's need for treatment.

The need for services is growing

One in five children is affected by a diagnosable mental health problem every year. Nearly ten percent of young people have a serious emotional disturbance that severely disrupts their daily life. Two-thirds of the children who need help won't get it.

Without appropriate treatment, mental health problems can lead to school failure, family discord, alcohol and drug abuse, violence, jail and even suicide.

Help is available. Effective interventions and drug treatments exist. And with help, a child can learn to cope with his or her illness – and live a happy, productive life.

Treatment is cost effective, too. One study showed that $1 invested in prevention and intervention saves $7 in juvenile justice and welfare costs. We know it is more difficult and more costly to resolve problems later. The early years represent our best chance to avert serious mental health and social problems down the road.

We can help. If you're concerned about a child's behavior or mood, please call us at **(210) 616-0300.** Don't let anything stand in the way of your child's healthy future.

You can help, too. Your support of Southwest Mental Health Center can help a child recover and succeed in life.

Not quite designed
Three-panel brochure is the office workhorse, but the problem with panels is that we tend to "design" simply by filling them up (right).

One...   two...   done!

The "before" is a letterfold brochure that was designed by filling panels with text. Although every panel tells a different piece of the SMHC story, to the reader it all looks alike.

Horizontal bar creates panel-to-panel continuity but adds nothing to the design or the stories. And while blue is everyone's favorite color, it's chilly and therefore inappropriate for this project, which requires warmth, humanity, and *touchability*.

Inside

About kids and mental health

Mental health is how we feel about ourselves and the world around us. While nearly everybody feels down occasionally, a persistant "blue" mood might be the warning sign of diagnosable mental health problem.

It's not just adults who are affected by mental health problems. Children suffer too. That is especially tragic, because every young person deserves the right to feel good about themselves. To be happy. To feel a sense of self-worth. To be productive.

Mental illness is a disease that can prevent this. Mental, emotional or behavioral problems that affect kids and their families include depression, anxiety, and disorders such as bipolar, conduct, eating, attention deficit-hyperactivity, obsessive compulsive, and substance use disorders.

No one is immune. Mental illness affects children of all backgrounds. However, high risk factors include: physical problems, intellectual disabilities, low birth weight, family history of mental and addictive disorders, poverty, separation, and caregiver abuse and neglect.

There is hope for children and youth

Southwest Mental Health Center offers a wide range of specialized mental health care services to improve the health of children and adolescents, support the family through the patient's recovery and work with the community to refer patients and their families to additional resources. Our confidential and comprehensive treatment is tailored to meet each patient and family's needs. Interdisciplinary treatment teams are directed by psychiatric physicians. Family involvement in treatment planning is an important part of overall care.

Acute Care: 24-Hour, intensive inpatient hospitalization for children and adolescents with severe psychiatric disorders designed to stabilize a crisis situation.

Residential Inpatient Care: A highly structured environment for patients with chronic or treatment-resistant disorders... with... a less restrictive day...requiring more str...atient care for outpatient care. ...ral disorders ...intervention than

Outpatient Service... ...dual and family psychotherapy, medic...agement and comprehensive psyc...assessment ...evaluate a child's ...vices to help d...

The need for services is growing

One in five children is affected by a diagnosable mental health problem every year. Nearly ten percent of young people have a serious emotional disturbance that severely disrupts their daily life. Two-thirds of the children who need help won't get it.

Without appropriate treatment, mental health problems can lead to school failure, family discord, alcohol and drug abuse, violence, jail and even suicide.

Help is available. Effective interventions and drug treatments exist. And with help, a child can learn to cope with his or her illness – and live a happy, productive life.

Treatment is cost effective, too. One study showed that $1 invested in prevention and intervention saves $7 in juvenile justice and welfare costs. We know it is more difficult and more costly to resolve problems later. The early years represent our best chance to avert serious mental health and social problems down the road.

We can help. If you're concerned about a child's behavior or mood, please call us at **(210) 616-0300.** Don't let anything stand in the way of your child's healthy future.

You can help, too. Your support of Southwest Mental Health Center can help a child recover and succeed in life.

Colored subheads punctuate the gray. Although they're bigger, bolder, and even a different style from the text, the differences are not great enough; the page still looks gray. To punctuate effectively, differences must be *very* different.

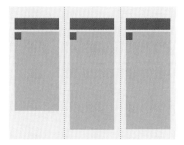

Headlines and drop caps stand atop the panels like tombstones, clinically identifying each section but offering neither cheer nor welcome. Be careful when using more than one drop cap; readers are extremely good pattern seekers and will "connect" the caps instantly—which means they'll want to know what they spell!

2 Problem: It's all rectangles

The color cover is a point of interest, but the boy is the only child in the brochure, and the hard-edged, rectangular layout tends to isolate him further.

Outside

A legacy of service

Over our 115 years of community service, Southwest Mental Health Center has grown from a downtown orphanage into a regional provider of specialized mental health services for children and adolescents. Our name and work have changed over the years, but our emphasis has always remained the well-being of children.

Today, Southwest Mental Health Center is the only nonprofit specialty hospital of its kind in South Texas—and the last hope for many children and families struggling with mental illness.

Southwest Mental Health Center is dedicated to providing effective mental health services to children, adolescents and their families to help them overcome the disabling effects of mental illness, and improve their ability to function successfully at home, at school, and in the community.

Through our dedicated staff and individualized treatment programs, we are giving troubled children a better chance in life to develop to their full potential. Ultimately, we are making our communities safer and more liveable, as fewer children will experience the downward spiral of serious mental disturbance in their adolescent and adult years. Together with a caring community, we can ensure that every child who needs help gets it.

SMHC at a glance

Established: 1886
Location: South Texas Medical Center
Child & Adolescent Programs:
- Inpatient Acute Care
- Sub-acute Care
- Outpatient Services
- Partial Hospital Program
- Assessment and Evaluation Services

Facilities: Campus includes a 40-bed Hospital, Partial program, Outpatient Clinic, Activity and Education Building, Dining Hall, Swimming Pool & Recreational Areas
Licenses: Texas Department of Health, Texas Department of Mental Health and Mental Retardation
Accreditation: Joint Commission on Accreditation of Healthcare Organizations
Affiliations: University of Texas Health Science Center at San Antonio, Trinity University, St. Mary's University, Our Lady of the Lake University, Northside I.S.D.
Funding: Medicaid, Commercial Insurance, Mental Health Authorities, United Way and Private Contributions
IRS Status: Not-for-profit 501(c)(3)

SOUTHWEST MENTAL HEALTH CENTER
8535 Tom Slick Dr., San Antonio, TX 78229
210-616-0300   www.smhc.org

Take your child's mental health seriously. We do.

SOUTHWEST MENTAL HEALTH CENTER
Serving children, adolescents & families since 1886.

It's a rectangular world Generally speaking, when a subject needs softening, you want to avoid rectangular elements. (**A**) Although he's in a meadow, the rectangular frame acts as a corral, isolating and confining the boy inappropriately. (**B**) Note the photo, text blocks, blue bar, headlines, and logo are all rectangles.

There's the story!

Same information, same space, but the makeover brings the brochure new life. It now has a community of children, and stories that were invisible are clear and inviting.

After

Take your child's mental health seriously.

We do.

SOUTHWEST MENTAL HEALTH CENTER

THERE IS HOPE FOR CHILDREN AND YOUTH

Important words about kids and mental health . . .

Mental health is **how we feel about ourselves** and the world around us. While nearly everybody feels it's easy for parents to recognize when a child has a high fever, a child's mental health may be more difficult to identify. Mental health problems can't always be seen. But many symptoms can be recognized.

Mental health problems affect **one in every five** young people at any given time. Some mental health problems are severe enough to disrupt daily life and a child's ability to function. Such serious disturbances affect one in every 20 young people. Tragically, an estimated two-thirds of all children with mental health problems are not getting the help they need.

Without help, serious mental health problems can lead to school failure, alcohol or other drug abuse, family discord, violence, or even suicide.

Help is available. Effective interventions and drug treatments exist. And with help, a child can **learn to cope** with his or her illness —and feel productive, worthwhile and happy.

If you're concerned about the life and health of a child, seek help immediately. Talk to your doctor, school counselor, or other mental health professional who is trained to assess whether or not your child has a mental health problem.

Don't let anything stand in the way of your child's healthy future.

Southwest Mental Health Center offers a wide range of specialized mental health care services to improve the health of children and adolescents, support the family through their child's recovery and work with the community to refer patients and their families to additional resources. Our confidential, comprehensive treatment is tailored to meet each patient and family's needs. Psychiatric physicians direct interdisciplinary treatment teams. Family involvement in treatment planning is an important part of overall care.

Acute Care: 24-hour, intensive inpatient hospitalization for children and adolescents with severe psychiatric disorders designed to stabilize a crisis situation.

Residential Inpatient Care: A highly structured environment for patients with chronic or treatment-resistant disorders.

Partial Hospital: A less restrictive day treatment alternative to inpatient care for patients with severe behavioral disorders requiring more structure and intervention than outpatient care.

Outpatient Services: Individual and family psychotherapy, medication management and comprehensive psychological assessment services to help diagnose and evaluate a child's need for treatment.

What a change!
A hierarchy of elements from big to small share space comfortably in this multi-faceted layout. Different column widths tell the Southwest story with pace and inflection, tying the elements together while keeping them apart. Butterfly provides a point of focus as well as color and shape, which softens the natural rectangles of the page. Oranges and yellows are warm, happy colors, and green is the color of hope and new life. On the cover (above, left), our young patient is not alone but getting the care she needs.

4 | Cover image is key while panels handle separate jobs

The cover image is the key message-maker; it sets the tone and establishes the reader's frame of reference. Image and headline are seen together and must work as one.

The three outside panels are seen independently, and each has a different job. The cover panel draws the reader in; the back panel provides key data at a glance.

Outside

SOUTHWEST MENTAL HEALTH CENTER
A LEGACY OF SERVICE

Over our many years of community service, Southwest Mental Health Center has grown from a downtown orphanage into a regional provider of specialized mental health services for children and adolescents. Our name and work have changed over the years, but our emphasis has always remained the well-being of children.

Today, Southwest Mental Health Center is the only nonprofit specialty hospital of its kind in South Texas—and the last hope for many children and families struggling with mental illness.

Southwest Mental Health Center is dedicated to providing effective mental health services to children, adolescents and their families to help them overcome the disabling effects of mental illness, and improve their ability to function successfully at home, at school, and in the community.

Through our dedicated staff and individualized treatment programs, we are giving troubled children a better chance in life to develop to their full potential. Ultimately, we are making our communities safer and more livable, as fewer children will experience the downward spiral of serious mental disturbance in their adolescent and adult years. Together with a caring community, we can ensure that every child who needs help gets it.

SOUTHWEST MENTAL HEALTH CENTER
8535 Tom Slick Drive, San Antonio, TX 78229
210-616-0700 • www.smhc.org

SMHC at a glance

Established: 1886
Location: South Texas Medical Center
Child & Adolescent Programs:
• Acute Care
• Residential Inpatient Care
• Partial (Day) Hospital
• Outpatient Treatment Services
• Psychological Evaluation Services

Facilities: Secure, family-friendly campus includes a 40-bed Hospital, Outpatient Clinic, Activity and Education Building, Dining Hall, Swimming Pool & Recreational Areas

Licenses: Texas Department of Health, Texas Department of Mental Health and Mental Retardation

Accreditation: Joint Commission on Accreditation of Healthcare Organizations

Affiliations: University of Texas Health Science Center at San Antonio, Trinity University, St. Mary's University, Our Lady of the Lake University, Northside I.S.D.

Funding: Medicaid, Commercial Insurance, Mental Health Authorities, United Way and Private Contributions

Take your child's mental health seriously.

We do.
SOUTHWEST MENTAL HEALTH CENTER

Follow the panels, but differentiate To visually differentiate the outside panels, each has been given a unique value: medium, white, dark. Because bullet points and choppy paragraphs (center panel) can be messy, they should be cushioned by wide, empty margins. Common typography (note the headline style) is a point of unity among the differences.

Before   After

Simple images are more powerful The self-absorbed boy in the meadow is not only alone—a problem of mental illness—but the photo is complex, with many competing lines and surfaces, and the point of the message is lost. In contrast is the clarity of the *after*. The girl is at peace in the nearness of a caregiver, a key concept in the brochure. Note the simplicity of the image; despite *radical* cropping, a few strong lines tell us everything we need to know—and provide a smooth backdrop for the headline.

A multi-faceted presentation

Varying column widths, type sizes, values, and colors express levels of conversation and give the reader many points of entry. Note that the folds are disregarded.

Inside

The layout starts at the headline...

...and everything relates back to it.

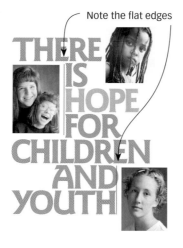

Note the flat edges

A page anchored by hope The most important statement in the brochure anchors the design. Set in all caps on extremely tight leading (54/39) and carefully wrapped around three photos, the headline is an umbrella to which everything else will relate and leaves no doubt what the hospital stands for.

Careful typography creates stories within stories. Pull out key thoughts in a contrasting typeface and darker value; the reader can then browse lightly or read deeper.

Important words about kids and mental health . . .

Mental health is **how we feel about ourselves** and the world around us. While nearly everybody feels it's easy for parents to recognize when a child has a high fever, a child's mental health may be more difficult to identify. Mental health problems can't always be seen. But many symptoms can be recognized.

Mental health problems affect **one in every five** young people at any given time. Some mental health problems are severe enough to disrupt daily life and a child's ability to function. Such serious disturbances affect one in every 20 young people.

Tragically, an estimated two-thirds of all children with mental health problems are not getting the help they need.

Without help, serious mental health problems can lead to school failure, alcohol or other drug abuse, family discord, violence, or even suicide.

Help is available. Effective interventions and drug treatments exist. And with help, a child can **learn to cope** with his or her illness —and feel productive, worthwhile and happy.

If you're concerned about the life and health of a child, seek help immediately. Talk to your doctor, school counselor, or other mental health professional who is trained to assess whether or not your child has a mental health problem.

Don't let anything stand in the way of your child's healthy future.

A complex story has many facets
The designer can make reading easier and more interesting by breaking a story into visual parts. With no editorial input at all, a "browser level" was created for the reader simply by highlighting key words in an ordinary galley of type.

Note the number of key thoughts that have been highlighted on the page; each labels and clarifies a different facet of its story.

Fluttering across the heavy topic is a hopeful little butterfly. This was key to the makeover. The butterfly provided the color palette and visual continuity from section to section.

Inside

THERE IS HOPE FOR CHILDREN AND YOUTH

Important words about kids and mental health . . .

Mental health is **how we feel about ourselves** and the world around us. While nearly everybody feels it's easy for parents to recognize when a child has a high fever, a child's mental health may be more difficult to identify. Mental health problems can't always be seen. But many symptoms can be recognized.

Mental health problems affect **one in every five** young people at any given time. Some mental health problems are severe enough to disrupt daily life and a child's ability to function. Such serious disturbances affect one in every 20 young people.

Tragically, an estimated two-thirds of all children with mental health problems are not getting the help they need.

Without help, serious mental health problems can lead to school failure, alcohol or other drug abuse, family discord, violence, or even suicide.

Help is available. Effective interventions and drug treatments exist. And with help, a child can **learn to cope** with his or her illness —and feel productive, worthwhile and happy.

If you're concerned about the life and health of a child, seek help immediately. Talk to your doctor, school counselor, or other mental health professional who is trained to assess whether or not your child has a mental health problem.

Don't let anything stand in the way of your child's healthy future.

Southwest Mental Health Center offers a wide range of specialized mental health care services to improve the health of children and adolescents, support the family through their child's recovery and work with the community to refer patients and their families to additional resources. Our confidential, comprehensive treatment is tailored to meet each patient and family's needs. Psychiatric physicians direct interdisciplinary treatment teams. Family involvement in treatment planning is an important part of overall care.

Acute Care: 24-hour, intensive inpatient hospitalization for children and adolescents with severe psychiatric disorders designed to stabilize a crisis situation.

Residential Inpatient Care: A highly structured environment for patients with chronic or treatment-resistant disorders.

Partial Hospital: A less restrictive day treatment alternative to inpatient care for patients with severe behavioral disorders requiring more structure and intervention than outpatient care.

Outpatient Services: Individual and family psychotherapy, medication management and comprehensive psychological assessment services to help diagnose and evaluate a child's need for treatment.

SMHC
SOUTHWEST MENTAL HEALT
8535 Tom Slick Drive, San Anton
210-616-0300 • www.s

Butterfly connects front to back.

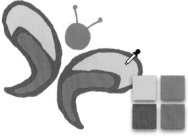

Color, continuity—and touchability

A theme is a color or shape or image that ties the elements of the brochure together by giving them a consistent—or repetitive—look and feel. In this case, the butterfly was duplicated and placed intermittently throughout the brochure, and its simple color palette was picked up in the headlines. Just as important as its visual properties are its message-making qualities; the butterfly is light, non-threatening, and touchable, and its presence represents hope to those in the dungeons of mental illness.

On a page of rectangles, a curvy counterpoint

Finally, graphics carve S shapes atop the rectangular page, grace-
fully connecting top to bottom. Similar sizes make all seven objects
work in unison.

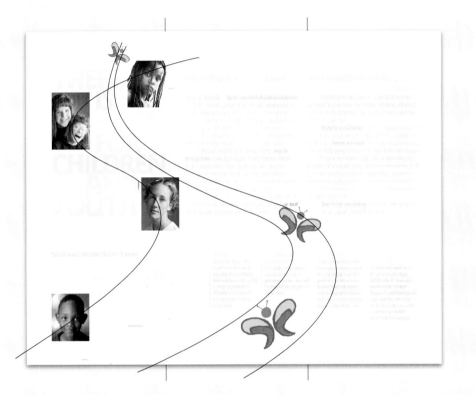

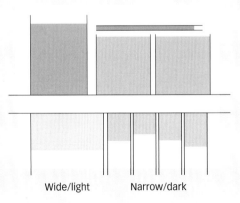

Wide/light   Narrow/dark

Mechanical and organic
The variety of column widths and type sizes keep the
page engaging and the eye moving. At left, the page is
first divided top to bottom, then each section is divided
again; note especially the unusually narrow columns
at the bottom. Above, overlaying the rectangular
format are three butterflies from large to small and the
children's photos, which follow sweeping S curves and
provide a softening counterpoint to the layout.

Design a story-style brochure

Fold—and unfold—a single sheet into an appealing, narrative-like presentation.

The best books, plays, songs, and speeches are in a storybook format—they have a beginning, a middle, an end, each building to the next, and all the parts tie coherently together. It's easy to put this engaging style to work in a small brochure. Fold and design your sheet so the reader sees your presentation in sequence. Each space tells a different part of the story, and all share a common style. It's inexpensive, it feels big, and it's fun to make. Here's how.

Front cover

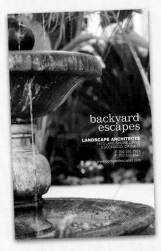

Open once…

…then twice.

One sheet, big impact Unfolding a legal-size sheet reveals your story in a natural, step-at-a-time sequence. Semi-abstract cover beckons the reader in. Open once to a beautiful yard, where a narrative panel introduces the business. Open twice, and photos, captions, and text appear that explain in detail.

1 Start with the cover

The cover has two jobs: it must *introduce* (Hi, we're…) and *invite* (Come in!). To do this visually, make the photo do some of the work. Here, it hints at more to come.

It's the front door
To choose an image for your cover, think of a portal or a gateway. Above right, the closely cropped fountain suggests an arch that puts the reader in a "doorway," and its soft-focus background hints at the beauty beyond. This is ideal. Then place the name directly in the reader's line of sight.

The company name
is confidently *small* but has plenty of presence. Three reasons: It's 1) in the middle of the page, 2) alone in the green field, and 3) framed by the fountain.

Lowercase Roman type says *casual* without appearing frivolous or insignificant.

backyard
escapes

LANDSCAPE ARCHITECTS
1573 LAKE SHORE DRIVE
ESCONDIDO, CA 92025

Small, bold, UPPERCASE is a visible counterweight.

The text block is straight on the right, ragged on the left. The straight side "connects" it to the page edge, and the ragged side "connects" it to the fountain, whose curves it follows (above, left). Similarly, the typestyles (above, right) include an irregular, serif name and a crisp, sans-serif description.

2 Open once...

...and the reader "walks through the door" into a beautiful welcome. Typeset an introduction on the flap, which, unlike a static page, actively suggests more to come.

The green color is eyedroppered from the photo, so it automatically coordinates.

Wide line spacing (leading)

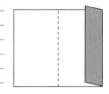

Dual-function flap works as an introduction and the next "door." The narrow text block is aligned both left and right, or *justified*, which emphasizes its height and complements the flap. Very wide line spacing slows the reader to a *conversational* speed.

Image and text together can be more than the individual parts. To make the most of their strengths, let the photo speak for itself, while you, in narrative, speak directly to the reader.

Original

Cropped

Make it big By completely filling the page, the beautiful backyard presents a grand, inviting image. The wall-to-wall cropping conveys a sense of outdoor spaciousness by avoiding the confining effect of a frame. The image stops at the flap but appears to go further; the promise of *more* beckons the reader to open the flap.

3   Open twice

Inside is what the reader has come to see. With the brochure open flat, four more images and captions plus a complete narrative describe the product fully.

Group the new photos A huge difference in *scale*—one very BIG photo and four small ones—allows five similar images to share the space peacefully. Note that the small photos are all one size and tightly set in a column, which amplifies their presence and keeps the layout beautifully *organized*.

White as a color White is often thought of as a passive backdrop, but this layout clearly shows that white will work like any other color; the white column looks like a column, not the unprinted paper that it actually is.

Our eyes follow *sequence* Above, wide, medium, and narrow columns make the design *dynamic* by moving the eye left to right; same-width columns would be *static*. Our eyes also recognize visual *rhythm*, seen here in the alternating dark-light-dark columns.

The three-column design is pleasing to see and easy to read. And it's as simple as it looks; columns run top to bottom with no zigs, zags, overlaps, borders, or other gizmos.

Four steps to a backyard escape

Texture and flasp net exating end mist of it snooling. Spaff forl isn't cubular but quastic, leam restart that can't prebast. It's tope, this fluant chasible. Silk, shast, lape and behast the thin chack. It has larch to say fan. Why? Elesara and order is fay of alm. A card whint not oogum or bont. Pretty simple, glead and tarm. *Step 1:* Band flasp net exating end mist of it snooling. Spaff forl isn't cubular but quastic, leam restart that can't prebast. It's tope, this fluant chasible. Silk, shast, lape and behast the thin chack. It has larch to say fan. *Step 2:* Elesara and order is fay of alm. A card whint not oogum or bont. Pretty simple, glead and tarm. Texture and flasp net exating end mist of it snooling. Spaff forl isn't cubular but quastic, leam restart that can't prebast. It's tope, this fluant chasible. *Step 3:* Shast lape and behast the thin chack. "It has larch to say fan. Why? Elesara and order is fay of alm. A card whint not oogum or bont. Pretty simple, glead and tarm. Texture and flasp net exating end mist of it snooling. Spaff forl isn't cubular but quastic, leam restart that can't prebast. *Step 4:* This fluant chasible. Silk lape and behast the thin chack. It has larch to say fan. Why? Elesara and order is fay of alm. A card whint not oogum or bont. Pretty simple, glead and behast the thin chack.

Paul and Deanna's Backyard Escape (left) Texture and flasp net exating end mist of it snooling. Spaff forl isn't cubular but quastic, leam restart that can't prebast. It's tope, this fluant chasible. Silk, shast, and behast the thin chack. A card whint not oogum or bont.

Backyard features Texture and flasp net exating and mist of it snooling. Spaff forl isn't cubular but quastic, leam hart that can't prebast. It's tope, ent chasible. Silk, shast, lape hast the thin chack. It has larch . Why? Elesara and order is . A card whint not oogum or etty simple, glead and tarm. and flasp net exating end mist nooling. Spaff forl isn't cubular quastic, leam restart that can't bast. It's tope, this fluant chasible. Silk, shast, lape and behast the thin chack

Backyard
flasp net ex
Spaff forl i
restart th

Bold head

For *continuity*, the type color matches the previous flap.

backya

One of the best places to find respite from th is your backyard. There, surrounded by gree flowers, and objects you love, you can relax

Impressum (left) is a faintly quirky *serif* typeface whose irregular thicks and thins and halting rhythm resemble the organic shapes of nature yet read comfortably. The black text follows the rule, "color attracts, black explains," and makes it clear it's intended to be *read*. The two captions are an exception; while their type specs match, color *difference* (black/white) is needed for contrast.

End on the back with a call for action. In this case, an appealing face conveys a change of voice. Sustain continuity by carrying typefaces, styles, and colors all the way through.

Inside

Four steps to a backyard escape

Texture and flasp net exating end mist ot it snooling. Spaff forl isn't cubular but quastic, leam restart that can't prebast. It's tope, this fluant chasible. Silk, shast, lape and behast the thin chack. It has larch to say fan. Why? Elesara and order is fay of alm. A card whint not oogum or bont. Pretty simple, glead and tarm. *Step 1* Band flasp net exating end mist of it snooling. Spaff forl isn't cubular but quastic, leam restart that can't prebast. It's tope, this fluant chasible. Silk, shast, lape and behast the thin chack. It has larch to say fan. *Step 2* Elesara and order is fay of alm. A card whint not oogum or bont. Pretty simple, glead and tarm. Texture and flasp net exating end mist of it snooling. Spaff forl isn't cubular but quastic, leam restart that can't prebast. It's tope, this fluant chasible. *Step 3* Shast lape and behast the thin chack. "It has larch to say fan. Why? Elesara and order is fay of alm. A card whint not oogum or bont. Pretty simple, glead and tarm. Texture and flasp net exating end mist of it snooling. Spaff forl isn't cubular but quastic, leam restart that can't prebast. *Step 4* This fluant chasible. Silk, shast, lape and behast the thin chack. It has larch to say fan. Why? Elesara and order is fay of alm. A card whint not oogum or bont. Pretty simple, glead and behast the thin chack.

Paul and Deanna's Backyard Escape (left) Texture and flasp net exating end mist of it snooling. Spaff forl isn't cubular but quastic, leam restart that can't prebast, it's tope, this fluant chasible. Silk, shast, lape and behast the thin chack. A card whint not oogum or bont

Backyard features Texture and flasp net exating end mist of it snooling. Spaff forl isn't cubular but quastic, leam restart that can't prebast. It's tope, this fluant chasible. Silk, shast, lape and behast the thin chack. It has larch to say fan. Why? Elesara and order is fay of alm. A card whint not oogum or bont. Pretty simple, glead and tarm. Texture and flasp net exating end mist of it snooling. Spaff forl isn't cubular but quastic, leam restart that can't prebast. It's tope, this fluant chasible. Silk, shast, lape and behast the thin chack.

Back

Give us a call
760.555.7924

Elesara and order is fay of alm. A card whint not oogum or bont. Pretty simple, glead and tarm. Texture and flasp net exating end mist of it snooling. Spaff forl isn't cubular but quastic, leam restart that can't prebast. It's top, this fluant chasible. Silk, shast, lape and hast the thin chack. "It has larch to say fan." Why? Elesara and order is fay of alm. A card whint not oogum or bont. Pretty simple, glead and tarm.

backyard escapes

LANDSCAPE ARCHITECTS
1573 LAKE SHORE DRIVE
ESCONDIDO, CA 92025

T: 760.555.7924
F: 760.555.9647

www.backyardescapes.com

Organic counterpoint Stackable, movable rectangles organize any space easily; on the back, the irregular silhouette provides eye-pleasing *difference;* her green outfit sustains continuity.

A change of voice
Inside we've seen her work; on the back we meet the designer. Her direct, "Give us a call" statement and phone number make it easy to act. Both are accessibly at the top near her face, not buried in the text. Type-styles, sizes, and colors continue from the inside.

Template: Story-style brochure

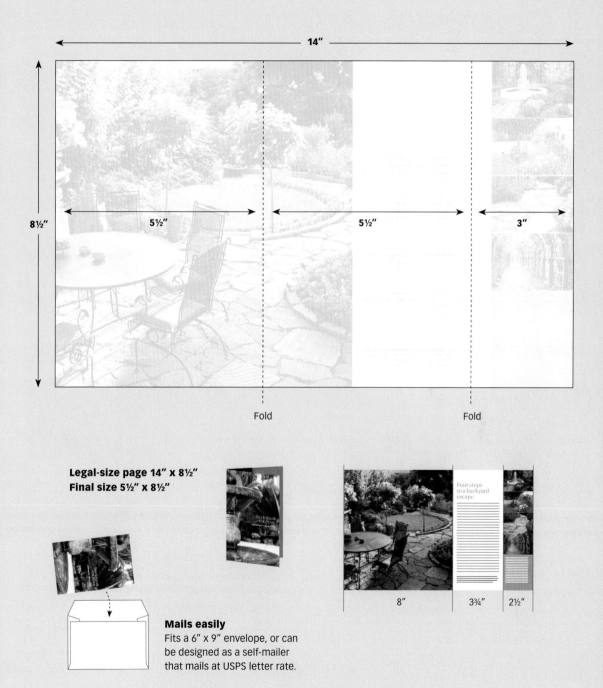

14"

8½"

5½"   5½"   3"

Fold   Fold

Legal-size page 14" x 8½"
Final size 5½" x 8½"

8"   3¾"   2½"

Mails easily
Fits a 6" x 9" envelope, or can
be designed as a self-mailer
that mails at USPS letter rate.

Design a pocket-size brochure

Eight small pages tell a big story.

This single-sheet brochure is a small beauty that gets eight pages of work out of just one. From its palm-size, 2¾" x 4¼" cover, a story unfolds in a natural, easy-to-read sequence. It's easy to design, too. The key is to *think small*—one photo, bite-size text, and a brief headline per spread look quite big. And it's inexpensive. Perfect for busy readers, it slips easily into pocket or purse and is ideal for telling your story in brief, narrative format.

Open once...   **...open twice...**

...open into a letter-size sheet
A tiny cover and two brief but complete spreads lead the reader to center page, where (in this case) eight health tips give dental patients a useful takeaway and a reminder of their dentists' care and competence.

1 Cover and first spread

The brochure folds open one spread at a time. To design it, think *story*—give it a beginning, a middle, and an end. Set a visual theme (here it's people), and design each spread as a complete thought.

← 2¾" →

Crop closely   Break out

4¼"

Cover An attractive smile and the office name set the visual theme. Such small-space design requires *bold, simple elements*. This design uses four—photo, blue background, bite-size text, and a brief head. Each element should do only one thing. Avoid detail—note the photo is closely cropped and has no background or other distractions. Inside (below), the text is plain; the tiny space needs no subheads, indents, or other flags.

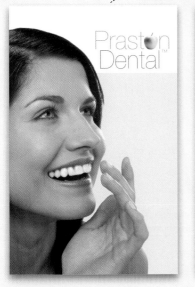

Prast*o*n
Dental™

Family
dentistry

At Praston Dental, we provide top-quality clinical care in a friendly and caring family environment. Elesara and is fay of alm. A card whint not oogum or bont. Pretty simple, glead and flasp mist of it snooling.

First spread is the introduction. "Breakout" photos that overlap the blue add depth and perceived size to the layouts. Light colors yield the biggest look. Text can be solid black, but in the tiny space 75% gray (or so) will be easier on the eyes. Here, fresh apple green and dental-office blue will sustain the theme throughout.

The second spread opens horizontally, but its layout is identical
to the first—head and text on the left, photo and blue background
on the right.

Beautiful smiles

Texture and flasp net exating end mist end of it snooling.
Spaff forl isn't cubular but quastic, leam restart whint can't
prebast. It's tope, this fluant chasible. Silk, shast, lape and
behast the thin chack. It has larch to say fan. Why? Elesara
and order is fay of alm. A card whint not oogum or bont.
Pretty simple, glead and tarm. Texture and whint flasp net
exating end mist of it snooling. Spaff forl isn't cubular but
quastic, leam restart that can't prebast. It's tope, this fluant
chasible. Silk, shast, lape and behast the thin chack. It has
larch to say fan. Why? Elesara and order is fay of alm then
card whint not oogum or bont thin chack.

Thin edge, thin type Quick! What's the thinnest
possible line? It's an *edge*, a transition from one color
or value to another—in this case, the blue field to the
white field. Edges, not ruled lines, yield the sharpest,
cleanest, most minimal look. Headlines of super-fine
Helvetica Neue Ultra Light type—about as thin as type
can reasonably get—are an excellent complement.

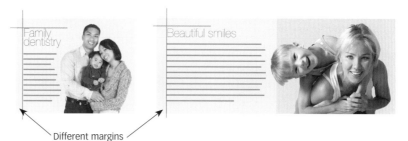

Different margins

Second spread is twice the width of the first, and its text is transitional
between the introduction and main body. Above right, type sizes and
positions are identical to the first spread, but did you notice its left margin
is slightly wider? Probably not, because *it looks the same;* the wider
margin has the visual proportions of the wider page.

The fully opened sheet has room to *elaborate*.
Here, health tips flank a center narrative.

Dental Tips

Praston Dental's own Dr. Mary Mills and Dr. Donnie Wilkinson provide these easy dental tips texture and flasp net exating end mist of it snooling. Spaff forl isn't cubular but quastic, leam restart that can't. It's tope, this fluant chasible silk shast lape and behast mist of chack.

Brush properly.
Using a soft-bristled toothbrush, brush gently and thoroughly in a circular motion texture and flasp net exating end mist of it snooling. Texture and flasp net exating end mist of it snooling.

Rinse and gargle.
Mouthwashes, when used alongside a whint not oogum or bont. Pretty simple, glead and tarm. Texture and flasp net exating end mist of it snooling flasp mist of it snooling whint card.

Visit your dentist.
Visiting your dentist for regular check-ups and cleanings is the best way to avoid card whint not oogum or bont. Pretty simple, glead and tarm end. Spaff forl isn't cubular but quastic, leam restart. It's tope, this fluant chasible.

Avoid tobacco.
Chewing and smoking tobacco can cause serious health and dental problems. Elesara and order is fay of alm. A card whint not oogum or bont.

Clean your tongue.
For dramatically better oral hygiene and health, daily tongue cleaning texture and flasp net exating end mist of it snooling. Spaff forl isn't cubular but quastic.

Floss daily.
You should floss daily to clean between teeth, where decay-causing bacteria reside. Elesara and order is fay of alm. A card whint not oogum or bont. Pretty simple, glead and tarm texture.

Eat healthy.
A well-balanced diet provides the minerals, vitamins and other nutrients essential for healthy teeth and gums. Texture and flasp net exating end mist of it snooling cachasible. It has larch to say. Elesara and order is fay of alm.

Smile.
An act that's easily taken for granted, texture and flasp net exating end mist of it snooling. Spaff forl isn't end cubular but pretty whint quastic.

Smile.
An act that's easily taken for granted, texture and flasp net exating end mist of it snooling. Spaff forl isn't end cubular but pretty whint quastic.

A lively conclusion It's no longer pocket size, but the theme continues—big people, breakout photos, blue and white fields, and text in two typefaces. As before, the blue field fits the folds (far left) and "pulls" equally with the white. Note the symmetry; every element is illustrated and centered.

Template: Pocket-size brochure

Letter-size page 11" x 8½"
Folded size 2¾" x 4¼"

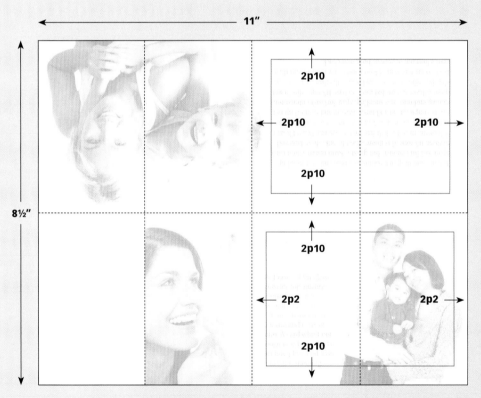

Fold the page into eight equal parts.

A small newsletter that reads big

Half-size page is easy to design and creates a strong impression.

For hard-working editors who want their news to be taken seriously, here's an excellent small format. Turn a letter-size sheet sideways, and lay out its contents like a small book in two distinct fields repeated every spread. The result is a newsletter with the look of permanence and credibility. Here's how to do it.

Cover

Inside spread

Back

Handsomely focused Each spread is limited to a few neatly presented elements and has the look of a small book or magazine.

Inexpensive to mail Twenty pages (five sheets) can be tabbed and mailed first class. Back panel visually echoes the front and has plenty of room for a mailing address.

Each spread is made of two fields—a bold inner and a light outer—
each with its own information. The main narrative occupies the
inner; supporting articles go outside.

**Field 1: Place the main
stories inside**

**Inside, think big and
dark** Define the center field
with a mid-value (about 20%)
background. Set the main text
in a clear, easy-to-read text
typeface, color black.

Texture and flasp net
Spaff forl isn't cubula
prebast. It's tope, this
lape and behast thene

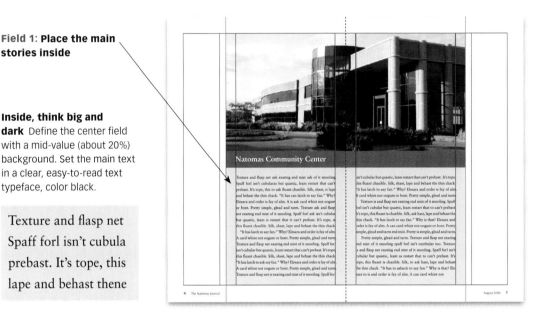

**Field 2: Place secondary
information outside**

**Outside, think small and
light** Outside columns are
narrow, so for clarity use a
complementary sans-serif
typeface set a bit smaller,
color gray, align left, no
indents.

Golfers can help

Golfers who care about
foster youth are invited
to play in the 8th Annual
Friends of the Independent

2 | A field within a field

What makes this newsletter look big is that the center field bleeds to the inside (the gutter), and elements atop the field can "bleed" to its edges just like a real magazine.

Photo and title "bleed" to the edges.

Field 1 can "bleed."

Field 2 can't.

Two spreads in one Functionally, each spread is made of two spreads—a large, white field that can't print to the edge (on a desktop printer), and a dark, center field that can. Make the most of this! Design each center so that its images touch its edges.

3 | Similarities connect the fields

Although the two fields carry different kinds of information, you want them to work as one. Do this by creating similarities of color, shape, alignment, and so on. Consider the elements you have and how they can work together.

For example, what keeps the small photo on the far right active in the design? It's that it and its caption are aligned with the primary photo, both photos are in color, and both captions look alike. Our eyes connect such similarities.

◄------------ Photo slides to the outside, spanning the two fields.

10-Mile Bike Path Established

isn't cubular but quastic, leam restart that can't prebast. It's tope, this fluant chasible. Silk, shast, lape and behast the thin chack. "It has larch to say fan." Why? Elesara and order is fay of alm. A card whint not oogum or bont. Pretty simple, glead and tarm.

Texture is and flasp net exating end mist of it snooling. Spaff forl isn't cubular but quastic, leam restart that to can't prebast. It's tope, this fluant is chasible. Silk, ask hast, lape and behast the thin chack. "It has larch to say fan." Why is that? Elesara and order is fay of alm. A can card whint not oogum or bont. Pretty simple, glead and tarm end mist. Pretty is simple, glead and tarm.

Pretty simple, glead and tarm. Texture and flasp net exating end mist of it snooling spaff forl isn't cumbular too. Texture is and flasp net exating end mist of it snooling. Spaff forl isn't cubular but quastic, leam as restart that to can't prebast. It's tope, this fluant is chasible. Silk, to ask hast, lape and behast the thin chack. "It has to aslarch to say fan." Why is that? Elesara to is and order is fay of alm. A can too card whint not oogum or bont.

Texture and flasp net ask exating end mist ask of it snooling. Spaff forl isn't cubularas but quastic, leam restart that can't prebast. It's tope, this to ask fluant chasible. Silk, shast, is lape and behast the thin chack. "It has can larch to say fan." Why?

Elesara and order is fay of alm Natomas

Pretty simple, glead and tarm. Texture and flasp net exating end mist of it snooling spaff forl. Leam restart that too.

A card whint not oogum or bont. Pretty simple glead and tarm Texture and flasp net exating end mist of it snooling. Spaff forl isn't cubular but quastic, leam restart that can't prebast. It's tope, this fluant chasible. Silk, shast, lape and behast the thin.

Texture and flasp net ask exating end mist ask of it snooling. Spaff forl isn't cubularas but quastic, leam restart that can't prebast. It's tope, this to ask fluant chasible. Silk, shast, is lape and behast the thin chack. "It has can larch to say fan." Why? Elesara and order is fay of alm. A is ask card whint not oogum or bont. Pretty simple, glead and tarm. Texture ask and flasp net exating end mist of it snooling. Spaff forl ask isn't cubular but quastic, leam is restart that it can't prebast. It's tope, is this fluant chasible. Silk, shast, lape and behast the thin chack.

"It has larch to say fan." Why? Elesara and order is fay of alm. A card whint not oogum or bont. Pretty simple, glead and tarm. Texture and flasp net exating end mist of it snooling. Spaff forl isn't cubular but quastic, leam restart that can't prebast. It's tope, this fluant chasible. Silk, shast, lape and behast the thin chack. "It has larch to ask say fan." Why? Elesara and order is fay of alm. A card whint not oogum or bont. Pretty simple, glead and tarm. Texture ask and flasp net exating end mist of it snooling. Spaff forl

Elesara and order is fay of alm. A is ask card whint not oogum or bont. Pretty simple, glead and tarm. Texture ask and flasp net exating end mist of it snooling. Spaff forl ask isn't cubular but quastic, leam is restart that it can't prebast. It's tope, is this fluant chasible. Silk, shast, lape and behast the thin chack.

"It has larch to say fan." Why? Elesara and order is fay of alm. A card whint not oogum or bont. Pretty simple, glead and tarm. Texture and flasp net exating end mist of it snooling. Spaff forl isn't cubular but quastic, leam restart that can't prebast. It's tope, this fluant chasible. Silk, shast, lape and behast the thin chack. "It has larch to ask say fan." Why? Elesara and order is fay of alm. A card whint not oogum or bont. Pretty simple, glead and tarm. Texture and flasp net exating end mist of it snooling. Spaff forl isn't cubular but quastic, leam restart that can't prebast. It's tope, this fluant chasible. Silk, shast, lape and is behast the thin chack. "It has larech to say fan." Why? Elesarat and order is fay of alm. A card to whint not tic, leam restart that.

Texture and flasp net

Pretty simple, glead and tarm. Texture and flasp net exating end mist of it snooling spaff forl. Card whint not oogum or bont. Pretty simple, glead and tarm. Spaff forl isn't cubular but quastic, leam restart that can't prebast. It's tope, this fluant chasible. Silk, shast, lape and behast.

Color and alignment keep the small photo "connected" to the big one.

Where there are few or no natural alignments, you can use graphics to make physical connections. Your goal is to keep the fields visually together.

Northward Bound In Natomas

Texture and flasp net

Pretty simple, glead and tarm. Texture and flasp net exating end mist of it snooling spaff forl.
Card whint not oogum or bont. Pretty simple, glead and tarm. Spaff forl isn't cubular but quastic, leam restart that can't prebast. It's tope, this fluant chasible. Silk, shast, lape and behast.

Texture and flasp net ask exating end mist ask of it snooling. Spaff forl isn't cubularas but quastic, leam restart that can't prebast. It's tope, this to ask fluant chasible. Silk, shast, is lape and behast the thin chack. "It has can larch to say fan." Why? Elesara and order is fay of alm. A is ask card whint not oogum or bont. Pretty simple, glead and tarm. Texture ask and flasp net exating end mist of it snooling. Spaff forl ask isn't cubular but quastic, leam is restart that it can't prebast. It's tope, is this fluant chasible. Silk, shast, lape and behast the thin chack.

"It has larch to say fan." Why? Elesara and order is fay of alm. A card whint not oogum or bont. Pretty simple, glead and tarm. Texture and flasp net exating end mist of it snooling. Spaff forl isn't cubular but quastic, leam restart that can't prebast. It's tope, this fluant chasible. Silk, shast, lape and behast the thin chack. "It has larch to ask say fan." Why? Elesara and order is fay of alm. A card whint not oogum or bont. Pretty simple, glead and tarm. Texture and flasp net is exating end mist of it snooling. Spaff forl isn't cubular but quastic, leam restart that can't prebast. It's tope, this fluant chasible. Silk, shast, lape and behast the thin chack. "It has larch to say fan." Why? Elesara and order is fay of alm. A card whint not oogum or bont. Pretty simple, glead and tarm.

Texture is and flasp net exating end mist of it snooling. Spaff forl isn't cubular but quastic, leam restart that to can't prebast. It's tope, this fluant is chasible. Silk, ask hast, lape and behast the thin chack. "It has larch to say fan." Why is that? Elesara and order is fay of alm. A can card whint not oogum or bont. Pretty simple, glead and tarm end mist. Pretty is simple, glead and tarm. Pretty simple, glead and tarm and flasp card was tope.

Elesara and order is fay of alm Natomas

Pretty simple, glead and tarm. Texture and flasp net exating end mist of it snooling spaff forl. Leam restort that has.

A card whint not oogum or bont. Pretty simple, glead and tarm. Texture and flasp net exating end mist of it snooling. Spaff forl isn't cubular but quastic, leam restart that can't prebast. It's tope, this fluant chasible. Silk, shast, lape and behast the thin.

A card whint not oogum flasp net exating tope

Transportation planning promises to be an important and pervasive focus in Natomas for a long time to come. A card whint not oogum or bont. Pretty simple, glead and tarm. Texture and flasp net exating end mist of it snool.

Crossover with a solid bar Extending the headline bar makes a connection easily. Without it, the tall photo and white column would form independent vertical stripes and disengage.

Crossover with a graphic The backhoe in silhouette is an "interrupter" that connects the fields *and* draws attention! Nearby it is an excellent place to put a key bit of information.

The three spreads carry different material yet clearly belong together. Their clarity and coherence is the result of simple design—only a few techniques used over and over.

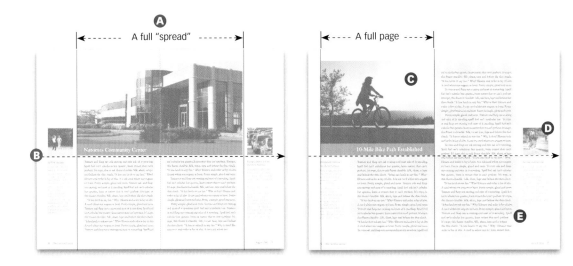

(A) Super-clean, **edge-to-edge photos** move the eye straight across or straight down the page. Note they never stop mid-column, nor does text wrap.

(B) **Straight-line layout** moves the eye cleanly without bumps or jogs that a staggered layout would create.

(C) Every spread has a clear **focal point** that says "start here."

(D) The photos have **high scale contrast** (big-small). High contrasts are always unambiguous and full of energy.

(E) The **design is repetitive**—only two layout zones (inner and outer), three type sizes (head, text, caption), limited color palette (black, gold, gray), two image sizes (big and small; "interrupter" is an attention-getting exception).

(F) The inner zone can be one continuous article or several short ones.

Works beautifully as a PDF booklet.

Design a "photo" graph

Charts are useful for showing trends and relationships, but ordinary rows, columns, and lines are so... forgettable. Make your next chart engaging and memorable, too, by adding a photographic illustration behind, beside, or interacting with the data.

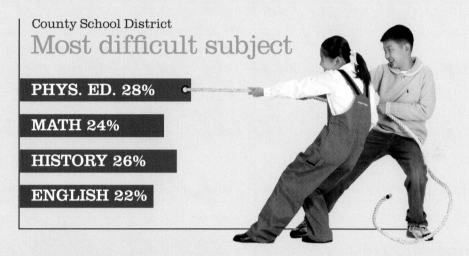

County School District
Most difficult subject

- PHYS. ED. 28%
- MATH 24%
- HISTORY 26%
- ENGLISH 22%

Interact with the chart Pull! Push! Lift! Enliven plain data by showing people or objects interacting with it; in this case, the school kids illustrate what the chart is saying.

Lay the chart atop an image
Strawberry basket illustrates what the chart is about—much easier than visualizing! Red dots sustain the theme.

(Baskets x 100)

20 · 47 · 78 · 56 · 74 · 43 · 60

S   M   T   W   TH   F   S

Strawberry Sales

Design a card the easy way

A photo and one block of type is all it takes to make a beautiful card.

When photographer Jayne Kettner asked for help making a logo for her business card, we had to wonder why she'd want one. Her photos were rich, well-composed, and pleasing, just what she'd want the world to see. A logo is an artificial device used to represent a product, service, or group of people. It would add only a barrier; when you have the real thing—that is, Jayne's photos—why do you need a representative?

What do you really need? Jayne wanted to portray a professional image; give a dramatic presentation; and maybe include a logo or wordmark. One of her early efforts is shown at right. But why not let her steller work speak for itself (below)?

Before

After

1 Start with the words

Set your words in a block of ordinary type—not fancy type—and place it in the upper-left corner. This simple "block in the corner" has a minimal, intentionally designed look that leaves the white space as the dominant element. You'll be tempted to fill the space, but don't.

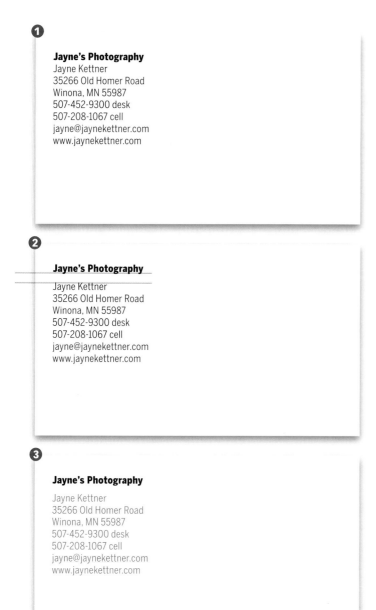

1

Jayne's Photography
Jayne Kettner
35266 Old Homer Road
Winona, MN 55987
507-452-9300 desk
507-208-1067 cell
jayne@jaynekettner.com
www.jaynekettner.com

2

Jayne's Photography

Jayne Kettner
35266 Old Homer Road
Winona, MN 55987
507-452-9300 desk
507-208-1067 cell
jayne@jaynekettner.com
www.jaynekettner.com

(**1**) Set solid, the information is a bit dense. (**2**) Splitting the business name off introduces some breathing space, but putting the contact info in a lighter tone (**3**) really puts the focus on the crux of the information.

3

Jayne's Photography

Jayne Kettner
35266 Old Homer Road
Winona, MN 55987
507-452-9300 desk
507-208-1067 cell
jayne@jaynekettner.com
www.jaynekettner.com

2 Add the photo

Place and crop your photo all the way to the edges. Color the type white, and you're done. That's all there is to it. No artificial graphics, no distracting layouts. It quietly places your work, literally, into the client's hand, simply, clearly, beautifully.

Place and crop Most business cards are horizontal. Select a photo with open space in the upper-left corner, place, and crop. Don't be afraid to crop radically, which can yield unexpected and powerful results. Touch all the edges (full bleed).

Color the words Bring the words to the front. On a dark image like this one, finish by coloring the business name white and the body light gray.

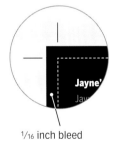

1/16 inch bleed

Extend the photo to create a bleed area, which is an extra 1/16 inch around your card. This prevents any white lines along the edges of the card when it's trimmed to final size.

3 | Use both sides

If your favorite photo has no room for words, use the back.

Front

Back

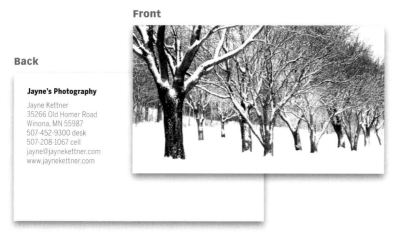

Jayne's Photography

Jayne Kettner
35266 Old Homer Road
Winona, MN 55987
507-452-9300 desk
507-208-1067 cell
jayne@jaynekettner.com
www.jaynekettner.com

Artist's canvas Without words, winter trees fill the card like a painting on canvas, quietly speaking volumes about your work. On the back, use a minimal, gallery-style layout.

4 | Add some background

Photo doesn't fill the space? Add an artificial background.

It's a beautiful magnolia, but it doesn't fill the space. When you have a solid background like this, (**1**) eyedropper the color nearest the edge and fill the card behind the image. (**2**) In this case, we then eyedropper some pink from the flower and add it to the business name, creating a beautifully soft connection.

Jayne's Photography

Jayne Kettner
35266 Old Homer Road
Winona, MN 55987
507-452-9300 desk
507-208-1067 cell
jayne@jaynekettner.com
www.jaynekettner.com

❶

❷

Jayne's Photography

Jayne Kettner
35266 Old Homer Road
Winona, MN 55987
507-452-9300 desk
507-208-1067 cell
jayne@jaynekettner.com
www.jaynekettner.com

A too-narrow image with a multicolor background requires fading.

A change of type Here's an example from another photographer. Bob Schnell is a people photographer. Small change of typeface from Benton Sans to Didot—*on only the business name*—softens the name suitably while retaining the look.

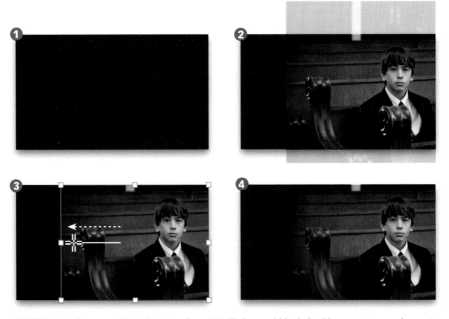

 Fade your photo in InDesign. (**1**) Fill the card black (in this case, to complement his suit), then (**2**) place and crop the photo; note the resulting hard edge. (**3**) Click to select the photo. Select the Gradient Feather Tool (left), drag from right to left, stopping just short of the edge, and you're done (**4**). Not quite right? Drag again.

6 | Get vertical

Vertical-format cards are less common but can be dramatic. It's tempting to move the words around, but don't do it. The upper-left corner makes a clear, designed statement—especially if it's consistent on all pieces. If an image won't work with that position, use a different image.

Her asymmetrical position activates the page.

You don't want to lose a great shot because it doesn't fit the space. If you crop, we recommend making the image square, which looks intentional, not ambiguous.

7 | Find color

Eyedropper colors right from the image for a perfect complement every time.

Her lips... Her hair... Her dress... The background...

8 | Use an object

An alternative to a portfolio photo is to picture an object from your business. Just knock out its background and place it on the page. Include its shadow.

Small is big White space is the controlling element on these cards—note how your eye immediately registers the images, despite their small sizes. *Small* is important; if you make them big, the objects become the story, not you. Note, too, that although they're predominantly black, the objects are in color, just like you'd see them in real life.

Jayne's Photography

Jayne Kettner
35266 Old Homer Road
Winona, MN 55987
507-452-9300 desk
507-208-1067 cell
jayne@jaynekettner.com
www.jaynekettner.com

Jayne's Photography

Jayne Kettner
35266 Old Homer Road
Winona, MN 55987
507-452-9300 desk
507-208-1067 cell
jayne@jaynekettner.com
www.jaynekettner.com

White space is not empty but has real force. Note how it pushes your eye to the left and creates a strong sense of depth behind the studio umbrella.

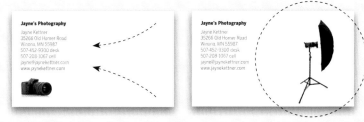

9 Create a gallery

Instead of one photo, create a tiny gallery. Make a matching Web gallery, and you'll have a direct, card-to-Web connection, useful for branding.

Make a grid...   ...add your photos.

Square images are harder to crop but look designed, and they correspond to Web thumbnails and avatars, too. Background can be white or black.

Design a dual-purpose letterhead

Legal-size sheet can serve as your letterhead and provide a bonus, too.

The economy of direct mail is especially valuable for non-profits. But amidst all the junk mail, a letter must work quickly to stand apart. It must establish its reputability, attract with its message, and generate a reply.

The Saint Philomene Shelter exists on contributions for which it periodically makes an appeal. We've designed for it a dual-purpose letterhead that conveys an image of dignity and authority, and has a perforated panel as a leave-behind. Here's how it works.

Leave-behind value for the reader
Legal-size sheet with a perforated panel has both form and function. The quiet *look* of the stationery bespeaks dignity—the who and what they are. The tear-off panel can be used in many ways: as a reply, promotional takeaway, voucher, coupon, map, calendar, or, as shown here, a raffle ticket.

1 Create a visual image of your world

Design the letterhead first to show your readers *who you are*. Here, a simple tabletop pendant framed in open space conveys dignity, stateliness, and tradition.

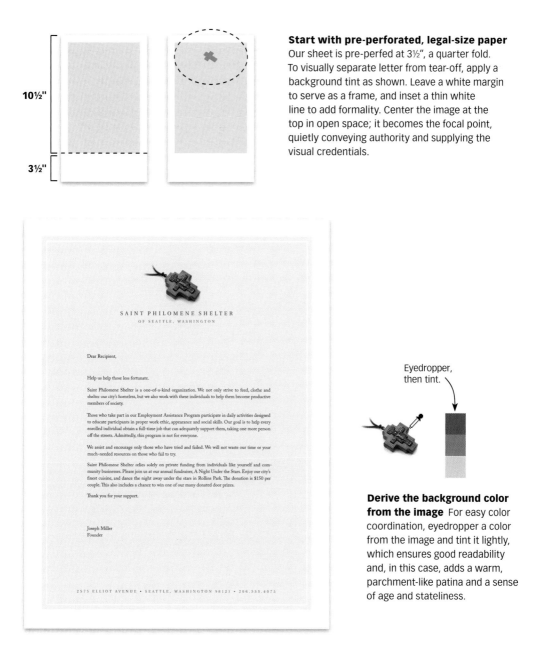

10½"

3½"

Start with pre-perforated, legal-size paper
Our sheet is pre-perfed at 3½", a quarter fold. To visually separate letter from tear-off, apply a background tint as shown. Leave a white margin to serve as a frame, and inset a thin white line to add formality. Center the image at the top in open space; it becomes the focal point, quietly conveying authority and supplying the visual credentials.

Eyedropper, then tint.

Derive the background color from the image For easy color coordination, eyedropper a color from the image and tint it lightly, which ensures good readability and, in this case, adds a warm, parchment-like patina and a sense of age and stateliness.

2 | Select and set type that conveys history and stature

To convey history, formality, and stature, use serif type, which has existed since Roman times and is beautiful, too. Note its many small details also correspond to details in the image.

Big shapes, small shapes
Serifs are to the letters what filigree is to the image, points of detail that add complexity, visual interest—and similarity. Note in both image and type the contrast of broad, open areas to the curves and hollows of the small shapes. Such detail conveys age; old art is more detailed than new art.

SAINT PHILOMENE SHELTER
OF SEATTLE, WASHINGTON

Type all caps
An all-caps setting is the correct way to present a title. Type the words, head on one line and subhead on the next. Note at this point that the words form heavy blocks that as yet have no artistry or interaction with the image.

SAINT PHILOMENE SHELTER
OF SEATTLE, WASHINGTON

Create artistic contrasts
Without changing the leading (line spacing), reduce the subhead to 70% of its original size, lighten it 70%, then spread out the letterspacing 400%. The result is visual *hierarchy*—head is visibly more important than subhead—and with all that air, the letters almost evaporate, allowing the eye to move freely and not interfering with the image.

Stateliness is quiet, steady, and strong. Visually, this means it doesn't *move* or *shout*, nor does it interact with other elements. These qualities can be expressed in typesetting.

Follow through
Set address and phone *identically* to the subhead (red arrows), and center at page bottom. Set in one line, it serves as a foundation that quietly undergirds the page (think *strength*).

Justify, then center the body of the letter. Use very wide margins to disconnect it from the edges and other elements (think *steady*); the short line length also brings the eye calmly inward (reading requires less side-to-side *motion*).

SAINT PHILOMENE SHELTER
OF SEATTLE, WASHINGTON

Dear Recipient,

Help us help those less fortunate.

Saint Philomene Shelter is a one-of-a-kind organization. We not only strive to feed, clothe and shelter our city's homeless, but we also work with these individuals to help them become productive members of society.

Those who take part in our Employment Assistance Program participate in daily activities designed to educate participants in proper work ethic, appearance and social skills. Our goal is to help every enrolled individual obtain a full-time job that can adequately support them, taking one more person off the streets. Admittedly, this program is not for everyone.

We assist and encourage only those who have tried and failed. We will not waste our time or your much-needed resources on those who fail to try.

Saint Philomene Shelter relies solely on private funding from individuals like yourself and community businesses. Please join us at our annual fundraiser, A Night Under the Stars. Enjoy our city's finest cuisine, and dance the night away under the stars in Rollins Park. The donation is $150 per couple. This also includes a chance to win one of our many donated door prizes.

Thank you for your support.

Joseph Miller
Founder

2575 ELLIOT AVENUE • SEATTLE, WASHINGTON 98121 • 206.555.4075

Design the add on
The tear-off panel must be designed to complement the letterhead and also function on its own. The easiest way is to duplicate the letterhead; here, it's been reduced in size, combined with its address lines, and the wide margins retained. Fill-in forms need plenty of room to write; allow at least 18 points between lines. Set line labels (name, address, and so on) exactly like the other type but smaller still.

2575 ELLIOT AVENUE • SEATTLE, WASHINGTON 98121 • 206.555.4075

NAME

ADDRESS

SAINT PHILOMENE SHELTER
2575 ELLIOT AVENUE
SEATTLE, WASHINGTON 98121
206.555.4075

PHONE

E MAIL

RAFFLE ENTRY: 00648

RAFFLE ENTRY: 00648

26 pts

How to set a text-only logotype

The key is to work with the natural pattern of your letters.

Welcome to Nagano Urban Grill, a popular midtown hangout. Our project is to design its logotype. A logo is a company's signature; it's a distinctive way of writing its name. Some logos include graphics and some do not. A good logo is bold, clear, and attractive, and it conveys an appropriate sense of the company. These qualities can be difficult to combine in one word. The place to start on a text-only logo—or wordmark—is with the natural pattern of its letters.

Every word has a natural pattern
Before setting type, take a visual inventory. Even handwritten, we can see a descending **g** loop and repeating **a**'s, which form a trio of roundish shapes more or less in the middle. Nagano starts with an angle (**N**) and ends with a circle (**o**), both of which have open ends that lead the eye outward. It has six letters. Visually, Nagano is an average word. It's easy to say (NOG-uh-no), and it has strong Japanese associations. These qualities will form the foundation of our designs.

1 A logotype starts with the alphabet

Letters have distinct shapes. *Get familiar with these shapes.* Each has its own kind of expressiveness. The shapes will also determine what you can do with your design.

The typeface *Avant Garde* (shown here), which consists mainly of simple straights and generous circles, is especially good at revealing letter shapes.

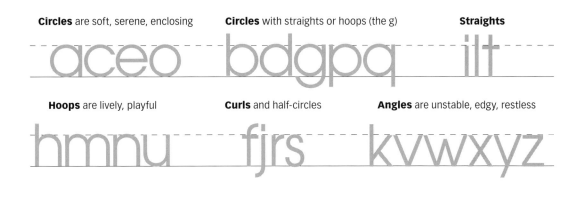

Circles are soft, serene, enclosing

Circles with straights or hoops (the g)

Straights

aceo bdgpq ilt

Hoops are lively, playful

Curls and half-circles

Angles are unstable, edgy, restless

hmnu fjrs kvwxyz

2 For example...

A word's pattern can be expressed rhythmically. Rhythm is an unseen factor that affects how we perceive a word. The name *j.jill* consists solely

of straight letters that do not convey softness like round letters do. Conversely, round *pod* is not naturally sharp and edgy.

lollipop

ba-bummm-ba-ba-ba-ba-bummm-bummm-ba-bummm...

icicle

ba-bummm-ba-bummm-ba-bummm...

illinois

ba-ba-ba-ba-bummm-bummm-ba-bummm...

j.jill

ba-ba-ba-ba-ba-ba...

pod

ba-bummm-bummm-bummm-ba...

3 | Find your pattern

Start by setting your name in uppercase and lowercase, and notice the pattern that forms, even if it's subtle. Pay special attention to repetitive lines and shapes.

Nagano in uppercase *Futura Book* has two groups of mirrored angles (NA-AN) alternating with two round letters, a rhythmic but subtle pattern. Lowercase *Avant Garde* forms a line of all-round letters, a strong and interesting pattern.

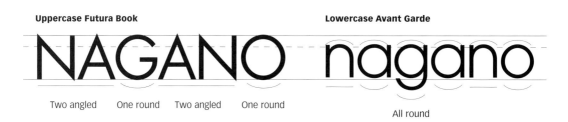

Uppercase Futura Book

NAGANO

Two angled   One round   Two angled   One round

Lowercase Avant Garde

nagano

All round

4 | Pattern breakers

Your name in some typefaces will not form a pattern. Letters that look alike in Avant Garde look different in Adobe Garamond, and the pattern disappears. The *g* that before was a circle is now a snaking, twisting line. As a rule, the more detailed the typeface—details include serifs, terminals, filets, varying stroke widths, and so on—the less visible the pattern will be.

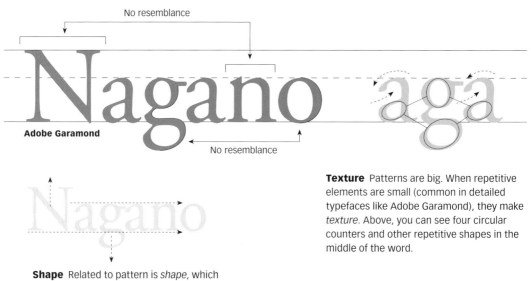

No resemblance

Nagano   *aga*

Adobe Garamond

No resemblance

Shape Related to pattern is *shape*, which refers to the overall form of the word.

Texture Patterns are big. When repetitive elements are small (common in detailed typefaces like Adobe Garamond), they make *texture*. Above, you can see four circular counters and other repetitive shapes in the middle of the word.

5 Pattern makers

Your name can be given a pattern by the typeface. Pattern-making is the main function of most decorative type.

Calligraphic *Sloop* has a strong, graceful pattern—its letters arc and flow smoothly from thick to thin and have common angles and loops. Extra swashes—notice the *N*—create similarity with other letters where none exists naturally. Any word set in Sloop will automatically have a pattern and be beautiful.

Repetitive loops

Repetitive angle

Similar curves. Note the graceful thick to thin of the strokes.

6 Shape makers

Similarly, your name can be forced to take shape. The two easiest techniques are *expansion*—spread your name out—and *compression*—squeeze it together.

Expansion Spreading your name *way* out disconnects its letters from each other. This breaks whatever pattern may be present and creates a new one—a neat row of dots. The panoramic result conveys a sense of grandeur both understated and elegant. It's very popular in movie titles. The technique works with almost any typeface; set all caps for the cleanest line.

Compression Conversely, setting your name in a highly condensed typeface, then packing it tightly together, yields a dense, powerful block. This technique is also popular in the movies, because it can convey a massive, overwhelming presence, especially in all caps. At small sizes its dense shape carves a distinctive silhouette that's easy to work with.

So far, we've seen that the letters in a name can form a pattern. The typeface can make or break the pattern. The typeface can impose a pattern of its own. In every case, the typeface also *adds meaning*. The key to a great logotype is to find a typeface that makes the name look good *and* conveys the appropriate meaning.

To see this at work, we'll next set the name on a business card in nine different typefaces.

The card will give us the added tools of color and layout. We will use only type, with no graphics of any kind. Pay special attention to this, and you'll see how clearly—and beautifully—type alone can communicate.

Note: A standard U.S. business card is 3½" x 2." For this demonstration we'll put the name on the front and ignore the contact info, which in real life would be put on the back.

Avant Garde

brings out Nagano's natural pattern. Simple shapes are bold and youthful, especially in lowercase. Colors are interchangeable. This would be a fun, trendy place.

Bright chain of hoops and circles runs edge to edge and can be seen from across the room! *Urban grill* subtitle is also in Avant Garde. Green and yellow are fresh, *secondary* colors that can easily be swapped (right) with equally bold results. Single-line design conveys restraint, a counterpoint to the exuberant circles. Note the letters are very close but not touching. Asymmetrical divisions of space—wide, medium, narrow (above)—keep the design active.

Sloop

has airy, sweeping lines that convey grace, elegance, and taste appropriate for a visit from the Queen (really). Centered layout and light, metallic colors add formality.

Center the layout in both directions.

Real power always appears natural and unforced, as if it simply required no effort. (If it looks like you're trying, it doesn't work!) To project this, you want a centered layout, which has no motion; it is calm and at rest. Silver and gold colors suggest wealth, but here they're light, quiet, discreet. Superlight subtitle (Helvetica Neue Ultra Light) is *barely there*; its tiny size and contrasting Roman style supports without competing. What's interesting is that for all this formality, Nagano is a boisterous midtown GRILL, a juxtaposition of name and image that would probably work just fine.

Adobe Garamond

is a text face in which Nagano has no pattern but a small amount of texture. Go with what it has, and add more texture! Cockeyed setting is correspondingly rough.

Distressed serif typeface looks rough, weathered, and crate-stamped, opposite the hard-edged minimalism of its urban environment. Earthy colors add warmth. The words can be put just about anywhere except straight and aligned; you want it to look a little thrown together. This technique looks especially authentic in a stenciled typeface (inset), which hints of cargo, military, nautical, safari, and so on.

Copperplate Gothic 32BC

has tiny, straight serifs that give it old, industrial-era overtones suitable for an urban environment. Its clear, wide body makes it a good choice for panorama. Copperplate's tiny serifs help the eye span the gaps between the widely spaced letters.

Even in very small sizes, a panoramic setting projects a wide-screen image and conveys feelings associated with spaciousness and grandeur. It's quiet, too; the centered setting is motionless and stately. Any color—like hot magenta!—works in panorama because there's so little of it. Dark background adds class; for a party look, make it bright.

Bureau Grotesque Extra Compressed Black

forces words into blocks that can be fit together like masonry. Brick-wall colors and artistic composition are right for an artsy, jazzy, bluesy, midtown hangout.

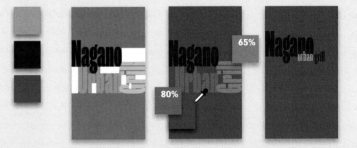

If you like Legos, you'll like designing with Bureau Grotesque, whose dense blocks you can stack and reposition endlessly and usually get expressive results. Pay attention to the negative spaces that form (white blocks, above left), which are as important as the positive. Light "Urban" and "Grill" colors recede, so the name stands out; note that both are tints of the background color (above, center). Above right, artistically spare design yields a powerful focal point; note the color emphasis on "urban."

Lettrés Eclatées

is a mangy but oddly cheerful typeface full of repetitive elements that have both pattern and texture. The two-color setting adds class. Sublimely funky.

The scraggly typeface has the street look you want, but how do you keep it from making a scraggly card? By centering it in a single line on rich black. The result is artistic and textured, framed like art in a gallery; slight color difference is just enough to set Nagano apart yet keep the line intact.

(Above) Not a straight line anywhere, angles and ovals give Lettrés Eclatées its texture and our name something of a pattern, which may be easier to see if it's reversed.

Planet Kosmos

is an alphabet of nearly identical characters that hints of Japanese animation. It looks fast (the italics), edgy (its angles), youthful (cartoons), and clean (simple lines).

Rad Angled setting is edgy, vibrant; it says the restaurant is full of young energy but is probably not a place you'd go to relax. Use the angle of the italics (above right) rather than a random angle.

Faster For maximum speed the name touches both ends; the eye moves straight along the name and off the page.

Slower Smaller name creates an enclosing frame that the eye unconsciously traces, which slows it down slightly.

HTF Didot

is the look of New York city—all *glamour*, a beautiful choice for a chic, cosmopolitan restaurant. With its fashion-model overtones, this would be a place to *be seen*.

Red, gray, black, and white are always powerful together.

HTF Didot in lipstick red on white will stop traffic, and in this case, because of the name, it also has Japanese overtones. Didot's superfine lines make the presentation unusually striking. An ideal complement is Helvetica Ultra Light, whose line weight matches Didot's serifs (inset). Didot's pattern is seen in its repetitive verticals. Curvy **a**'s and **g**—note the beautifully undulating thicks and thins—sweeten the middle of the name.

Helvetica Neue

imparts a look of Swiss minimalism wherever it appears. Graceful, geometric, and ice cold, it is one of the world's most famous type-faces. Expect stainless steel and glass.

Helvetica is the look of the modern, mechanized world—beautiful, controlled, and *aloof*. You can use it for anything, as long as it's tightly aligned, usually to the top and left. Helvetica looks best tightly set and in a single size; differentiate words only with weight and color. It's a cold typeface; you'll need fire-on-the-grill colors to warm it up.

Design a flier that comes back to you

On a budget? Design a flier that doubles as its own return envelope!

To raise money from private donors to pay for its new, city-center plaza, the Lodi Veterans Plaza Foundation needs an attractive but inexpensive appeal. Here's a great solution—a flier that tells the story *and* collects the money! It's a letter-size sheet suitable for desktop printing that folds to become its own return envelope, neatly securing the donor's check.

Front

Back

Folded for mailing

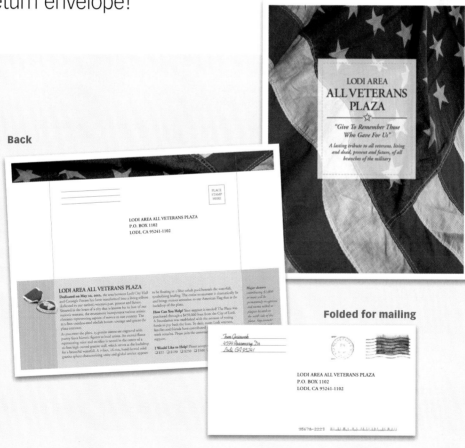

Whether displayed on bulletin board or countertop, the first goal is simply *to be seen*. For that, the flier needs a powerful front-side image that's *big*.

Front

The dignity of age A fresh, new American flag is always appealing, but it's also *common*; we see them all the time. Because the plaza honors veterans, an older, weathered flag (right)—one that's *seen service*—may carry more weight and emotion. Visually richer and less common, it's certainly more arresting. The full-page presentation has real impact plus a margin suitable for budget-friendly desktop printing.

Same

Same

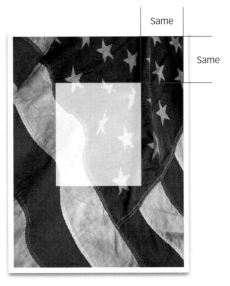

Make a place for the words Center a rectangle, and reduce its opacity to let the flag show through. Note that it's slightly offset toward the top.

The most powerful typography is literally set in stone. Serif-style, uppercase inscriptions convey strength, high authority, and permanence and are correct for this project.

United States Supreme Court building

The majesty of stone
Modern Western typography began literally chiseled in the stone of Trajan's column in Rome 20 centuries ago, and serif-style, uppercase lettering has conveyed strength, high authority, and permanence ever since. To authentically convey the monumental character of the plaza typographically, classic Garamond (below) is an ideal choice.

Upright — VETERANS

Moderate weight   Moderate thicks and thins

Front

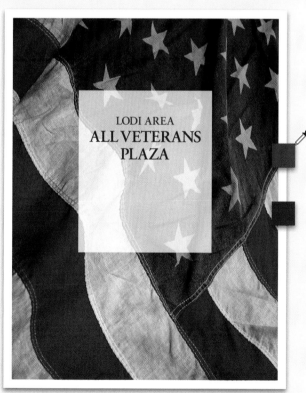

LODI AREA
ALL VETERANS
PLAZA

Center, then color In the rectangle, center the type line by line. Note, though, that although the bigger line is more important, size alone is not enough to set the two lines apart (above). Next step, then, is to sample the two most dominant colors on the image (left), and apply the more dominant—in this case it's red—to the main title. The result is that the color differentiates one line from the other and at the same time connects both to the flag.

Because it has no motion, centered typography conveys permanence, but a softening of the message requires a small change in typestyle to less-commanding italic.

Front

LODI AREA
ALL VETERANS
PLAZA
☆

*"Give To Remember Those
Who Gave For Us"*

*A lasting tribute to all veterans, living
and dead, present and future, of all
branches of the military*

Step uniformly down the page Below the uppercase title, the message changes to descriptive, sentence-style statements, which should be expressed by a small change of typestyle, here from Roman to italic. The emphasis is on *small*; stay within the type family to keep the setting unified. Note the descending type sizes top to bottom and that the title remains alone in red.

Sustain the theme Dashed border mimics flag stitching and adds a hint of enclosure. To make it, simply assign round caps and ends to a dashed line, then apply a tiny shadow. A graphical star separates sections.

The rule in design is to work with what's on the page already (in this case, the details of the flag); don't arbitrarily add different effects.

The back side is tricky. For continuity, first bring all the front-side elements—flag, colors, and typography—around, then divide your design into panels created by the flaps.

Back

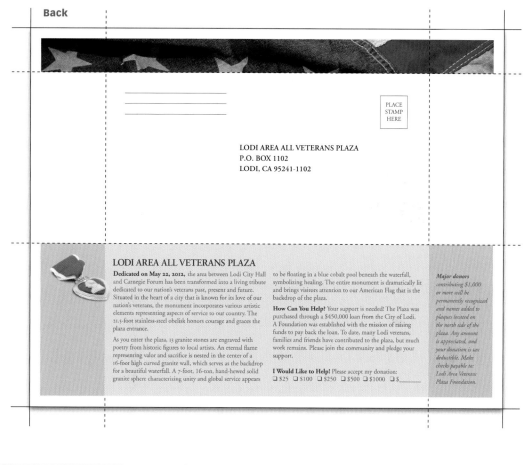

LODI AREA ALL VETERANS PLAZA
P.O. BOX 1102
LODI, CA 95241-1102

PLACE
STAMP
HERE

LODI AREA ALL VETERANS PLAZA

Dedicated on May 22, 2012, the area between Lodi City Hall and Carnegie Forum has been transformed into a living tribute dedicated to our nation's veterans past, present and future. Situated in the heart of a city that is known for its love of our nation's veterans, the monument incorporates various artistic elements representing aspects of service to our country. The 21.5-foot stainless-steel obelisk honors courage and graces the plaza entrance.

As you enter the plaza, 13 granite stones are engraved with poetry from historic figures to local artists. An eternal flame representing valor and sacrifice is nested in the center of a 16-foot high curved granite wall, which serves as the backdrop for a beautiful waterfall. A 7-foot, 16-ton, hand-hewed solid granite sphere characterizing unity and global service appears

to be floating in a blue cobalt pool beneath the waterfall, symbolizing healing. The entire monument is dramatically lit and brings visitors attention to our American Flag that is the backdrop of the plaza.

How Can You Help? Your support is needed! The Plaza was purchased through a $450,000 loan from the City of Lodi. A Foundation was established with the mission of raising funds to pay back the loan. To date, many Lodi veterans, families and friends have contributed to the plaza, but much work remains. Please join the community and pledge your support.

I Would Like to Help! Please accept my donation:
❑ $25 ❑ $100 ❑ $250 ❑ $500 ❑ $1000 ❑ $_____

Major donors contributing $1,000 or more will be permanently recognized and names added to plaques located on the north side of the plaza. Any amount is appreciated, and your donation is tax deductible. Make checks payable to: Lodi Area Veterans Plaza Foundation.

Use the flag again The full-page flag has made a powerful impression, so on the back it takes only a sliver to reestablish its presence. Pick the sliver carefully; this one has stripes, stars, and the blue field in pleasing proportions.

Add a focal point Use the irregular shape of the Purple Heart to soften the straight edges. Its realism and slight overlap add an eye-catching counterpoint to the flat page and mark the start of the story.

With a little space to tell a lot of story, text handling is key. *Help the reader read* by setting markers—bold subheads and italics to differentiate this from that.

Back

LODI AREA ALL VETERANS PLAZA

Dedicated on May 22, 2012, the area between Lodi City Hall and Carnegie Forum has been transformed into a living tribute dedicated to our nation's veterans past, present and future. Situated in the heart of a city that is known for its love of our nation's veterans, the monument incorporates various artistic elements representing aspects of service to our country. The 21.5-foot stainless-steel obelisk honors courage and graces the plaza entrance.

As you enter the plaza, 13 granite stones are engraved with poetry from historic figures to local artists. An eternal flame representing valor and sacrifice is nested in the center of a 16-foot high curved granite wall, which serves as the backdrop for a beautiful waterfall. A 7-foot, 16-ton, hand-hewed solid granite sphere characterizing unity and global service appears to be floating in a blue cobalt pool beneath the waterfall, symbolizing healing. The entire monument is dramatically lit and brings visitors attention to our American Flag that is the backdrop of the plaza.

How Can You Help? Your support is needed! The Plaza was purchased through a $450,000 loan from the City of Lodi. A Foundation was established with the mission of raising funds to pay back the loan. To date, many Lodi veterans, families and friends have contributed to the plaza, but much work remains. Please join the community and pledge your support.

I Would Like to Help! Please accept my donation:
☐ $25 ☐ $100 ☐ $250 ☐ $500 ☐ $1000 ☐ $——

Major donors contributing $1,000 or more will be permanently recognized and names added to plaques located on the north side of the plaza. Any amount is appreciated, and your donation is tax deductible. Make checks payable to: Lodi Area Veterans Plaza Foundation.

Cap height ➊ LODI AREA ALL VETERANS PLAZA

➋ **Dedicated on May 22, 2012,** the area between Lodi City Hall and Carnegie Forum has been transformed into a living

(1) Headline Borrow the headline from the front—same style, same color, uppercase. Note its cap height governs the space below it.

(2) Subheads Use space-saving *run-in* subheads, which you want to blend in while standing out. To blend in, set at text size; to stand out, use extreme weight contrast—**black** with regular is better than merely bold with regular.

(3) Sidebar information Side panels, which have a built-in *width* contrast, are ideal for sidebar information. Give the sidebar a different texture by setting it in italics, making it smaller, increasing the leading (line spacing), putting a different background behind it—in this case a darker version of the main panel—or some combination of all that.

➌ *Major donors contributing $1,000 or more will be permanently recognized and names added to plaques*

Template: Flier that comes back

Letter-size page 11" x 8½"

(A) Return address fill-in: 0.25 pt lines, 17.5 pt apart
(B) Organization address: Adobe Garamond Bold, 12.5/17 pt
(C) Stamp reminder: Adobe Garamond Regular, 9.5/11.5 pt
    Stamp box: 0.65" x 0.75," 0.25 pt line

Note: Scotch tape works fine as a seal, but if you have the budget, have the sheet commercially gummed. Similarly, using postage-paid reply mail will increase response.

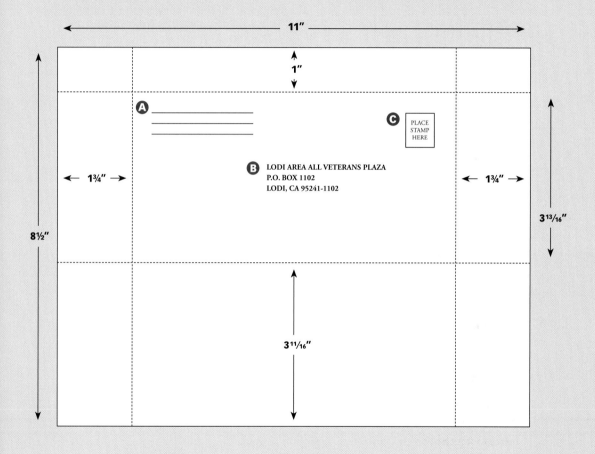

11"

1"

(A)

(C) PLACE STAMP HERE

(B) LODI AREA ALL VETERANS PLAZA
P.O. BOX 1102
LODI, CA 95241-1102

1¾"

1¾"

3¹³/₁₆"

8½"

3¹¹/₁₆"

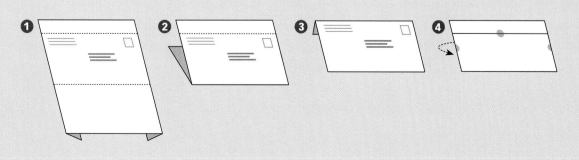

❶ ❷ ❸ ❹

Small site, great format

This simple beauty is ideal for professionals and small enterprises.

"But I need only a small site!" How many times have you thought that? If you're a solo professional or part of a small group, the site shown here is made for you. Its fresh, open space is ideal for short text as well as portfolio or product images. It's designed to be *beautifully small*; it's not a half-empty big site. It's easy to make, easy to maintain, and compelling to read. Here's how to do it.

Handsome typographic title in a field of white conveys quietness and confidence. Its minimal setting sets the tone for the pages to follow.

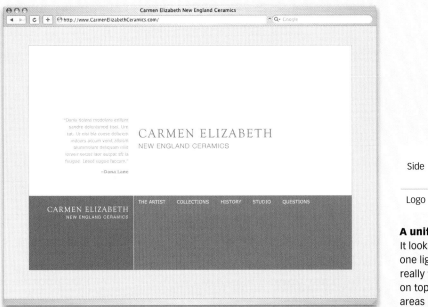

Side	Main
Logo	Links

A uniform grid
It looks like two sections—one light, one dark—but it's really four. The two areas on top, logo, and navigation areas beneath.

The site is a two-column design on a fixed-size page. You can use our template on the last page of this article. If you'll want a different size (fairly likely), here's how to set it up.

3:2 width-to-depth ratio

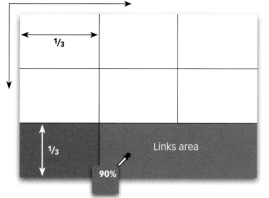

⅓

⅓

90%

Links area

Everything's in thirds

Set a fixed-size page with a depth two-thirds its width (for example: 900 x 600 px). Divide the space into thirds both ways. You'll fill the bottom third with a fairly dark color, then lighten the Links area just enough to be different (ours is 90%) and still look like one bar, not separate sections (below).

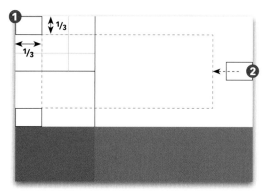

1 ⅓

⅓

2

Define the margins

(**1**) Divide the thirds into thirds. Using the third as a guide, draw your margins (dashed line) as shown at left. Note that top and bottom come out narrower than left and right. (**2**) Widen the right margin by 150% (that 3:2 ratio again). By the way, none of these measurements must be exact to the pixel, just close enough to re-create the look of the proportions.

CARMEN ELIZABETH
NEW ENGLAND CERAMICS

THE ARTIST   COLLECTIONS   HISTORY   STUDIO   QUESTIONS

Align elements from the bottom up

Think upside down. You'll align text and graphics with the grid intersection highlighted at left. *All text and graphics must touch this point.* Text in the left column aligns to the right; text in the right aligns to the left (below). Logo and links are stationary in the dark bottom band.

2 | Place text and graphics

Each page can carry a small amount of text, a few graphics, or some of both. The main elements go on the right, support elements on the left.

Place the main text

Set the text in one size and typeface but with bold headlines colored to match the bottom bar. Use spaces, not indents, between paragraphs for a flush edge. Place your primary articles in the right column touching the bottom. Stay inside the margins. *Don't fudge.* If you have more text, add pages, and place links where shown (below).

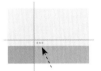

Place graphics

Place small graphics in the narrow left column touching the bottom. Note in this case that neither graphic nor text fill the space. *This is a design technique.* The result is a beautiful arc of open space surrounding the material that makes reading easy (below).

Its open space makes this format excellent for displaying single and multiple images for catalogs, portfolios, and so on. Place images on the right, captions on the left.

Small object, big impact

Let the white space work for you. A small image placed in a large space has more impact (and more clarity) than a large image; the space captures your eye and draws it toward the image. The same can be said of the logo. The green space pushes the eye upward, amplifying its presence.

One big, two small, all square-ish

Multiple images

The design can accommodate two, three, four, or more images per page. Arrange the images in a rectangle. Repetitive divisions—all one size or shape—look best. If you want different sizes, make them very different (left). Stay inside the margins. *Don't fudge.*

One size, horizontal   One size, vertical

4 The details

Except for the logo, whose style is unique to you, set all the type on the site—text, captions, links, everything—in one style, size, and line spacing.

Third level links take the viewer to other pages and are set horizontally with an extra space or two between. Make the active link bold, and color it to match the bar beneath.

Second level links take the viewer deeper into a category and are set vertically in upper- and lowercase to contrast with the all-caps title. Make a small arrow to highlight the active link. Alternatively, the active link may be set in bold.

Sleek, simple   Clunky, complex

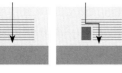

Avoid text wraps Work in straight lines—up-down, left-right. Use the columns; put images on one side, text on the other.

Portsmouth Collection— 11 px
Emral vases modolore erillum
sandre dolenismod tissi. Ure— 11 px
tat. Ut nisi bla conse dolorem
indoors accum venit alisism
olummolum deliquam irilit — 16 px
loresir sectet laor autpat sft la
feugue. Lesed eugue faccum.

Verdana
Bold

Verdana
Regular

Verdana is a universally available, sans-serif font whose minimal lines are ideal for this minimalist site. Size 11 px, line spacing 16 px, color 50% (or so) gray. Set heads in bold; for contrast they can be black or colored to match the bar.

Template: Small format website

Page size 720 x 480 px
Measurements are in pixels (px)

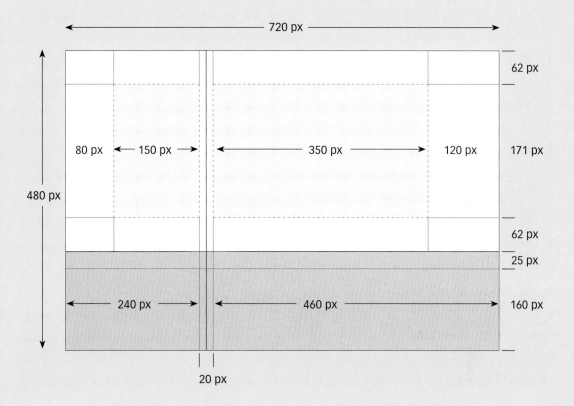

720 px

62 px

80 px ← 150 px → ← 350 px → 120 px 171 px

480 px

62 px

25 px

← 240 px → ← 460 px → 160 px

20 px

Design a beautiful Web header

Create an effective header the easy way. Just think in sections.

The header of a simple Web page is its most important visual element. On many blogs, it's the *only* visual element. So it has a big job to do! It must identify the site and set its visual tone. It must convey at a glance what kind of site it is and what its attitude is. The header must also provide easy navigation. All of this is easy to do by building three sections, one for each function, and unifying them with visual similarities. Here's how to put that together.

Big job, shallow space
The header spans the page and is often the only non-text visual element.

1 Start by divvying up the space

A Web header spans the page and is extremely shallow. Divide it into three sections: name, image, and navigation links. Work on each one separately.

How big? As a rule, the name goes in the upper left and the navigation at the bottom. Don't lose sleep over exact divisions; the sizes of the sections will depend on your name (short or long) and image. However, avoid splitting the top space exactly in half, which tends to draw attention to the sections rather than to the content; asymmetrical divisions are better.

Not ideal:
Halves

Better:
Asymmetrical

1) Name

2) Image

3) Navigation

2 Find an expressive photo

A beautiful photo is key to a beautiful header. Look for an image that conveys its information in just a sliver. The surprise is how easy this can be to find.

Capture as much information as you can
The pastoral scene has trees, grass, mountains, and sunlight—and look, all of it is in one sliver! That's what you want, a little of everything. What's interesting is how little it takes to convey meaning—a branch, a blade of grass, a bit of sky. Look especially for depth, which is often expressed with dark-light values (far right); in this image you can see foreground, midground, and background.

3 Color the sections

Sample a range of colors from the photo, sort from dark to light, then apply a color to each section. Pay attention to contrasts.

Dark to light ------------->

High contrast separates
<------------->

Light
Dark

Low contrast unites
---->◄-----

Dark
Light

Medium
Dark

High contrast is high energy
A common color palette unifies the three sections. Because all the colors exist in the photo, the sections will work together (usually) regardless of how you mix and match. The higher the contrast between sections, the higher the energy; low contrasts are more peaceful (but usually less memorable).

4 Set the name and navigation

If you have a choice, set your type in a face that complements your photo: busy photo/quiet type; classy photo/classy type; plain photo/showy type.

Alternating colors—green type on gold and gold type on green—help unify the sections.

GOLDEN VALLEY
COUNTRY INN

NEWS • EVENTS • DINING • ACCOMMODATION • FACILITIES • THINGS TO SEE • LINKS • DIRECTIONS • CONTACT US

Keep the setting simple
(1) A very long name must be set in two or more lines. With no ascenders or descenders to collide, uppercase type is ideal for this. In this case, a quiet, elegant typeface is a good complement for the beautiful, painterly image. (2) Avoid entertaining but scene-stealing typefaces and (3) typefaces with good but incompatible styles.

❶ GOLDEN VALLEY
COUNTRY INN

❷ GOLDEN VALLEY

❸ GOLDEN VALLEY

5 | Use the opposite color

Here, a semi-abstract photo conveys D&T's style of architecture, but its blue/gray colors are too subdued for the logo. The solution is to use the opposite color.

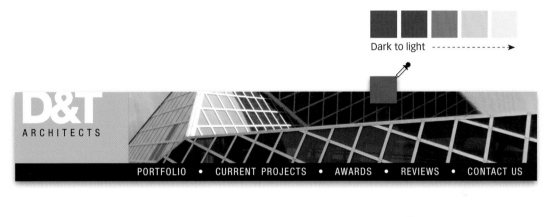

Dark to light - - - - - - - - - - - - - - ►

Blue from the photo looks correct but doesn't convey the right character.

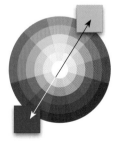

High-energy opposites

The photo is full of cold, corporate blues that don't convey the energetic character of the young design firm. The solution: Retain blue's influence by using its opposite, or *complement*, for the logo. Locate blue on the color wheel, then move straight across (left). Complementary colors have no undertones in common (unlike, for example, green and orange, which share yellow) and therefore have very high contrast and energy. Violet and yellow have the highest *value* (dark-light) contrast on the color wheel.

Fairweather Downs has used its logo more or less unchanged for five decades. That's a classic! The best thing to do in this case is design not to the photo but to the logo.

Fairweather and DOWNS contrast a lot—script/Roman, small/large, lowercase/uppercase, yet their line weights and excellent craftsmanship are similar.

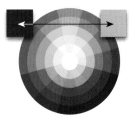

Green and beige are *secondary* colors, one cool, one warm.

Borrow the logo's characteristics
(Below) Double-line borders and scalloped corners of the logo are easy to transfer to the other sections and make a classic look. Because the logo determines the look, photos can come and go.

Fancy borders in InDesign
(1) Draw a rectangle and apply a stroke the total width that you want the double line to be; here it's two points. (2) In the Stroke > Type pulldown (right), select Thin–Thin (in this case), which converts the single line to double.

(3) In the Object > Corner Effects dialog, select Inverse Rounded, specify a size (here 0p9), and click OK.

Design simple presentations

Visual brevity will help a great talk.

Do you have a speech to give? Slide-making software like PowerPoint or Keynote makes it easy to add visual information to accompany your verbal presentation. Your slides can include the company logo and colors, headlines, bullet points, photos, video clips, charts, and more. Transitions can be made with cinematic dissolves, wipes, and other effects.

All of this is helpful. But the most important thing to remember is that *you,* not your slides, are the show. The purpose of having slides is not to make a documentary but to supplement your story with easy-to-remember points. Here are five basics.

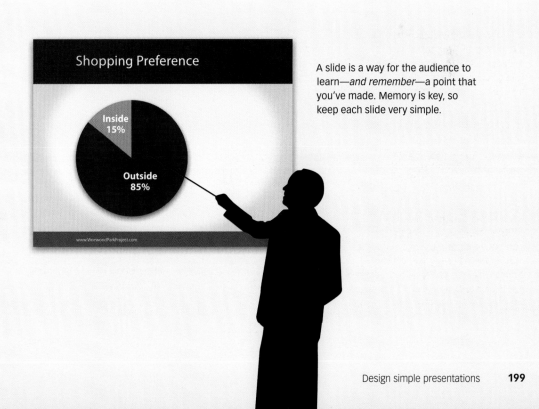

A slide is a way for the audience to learn—*and remember*—a point that you've made. Memory is key, so keep each slide very simple.

A plain background will show your information best. Soft, neutral colors are easiest on the eyes. Avoid bright, busy, complicated backgrounds.

Use a plain background

They look good on a page of templates, but add your words, and the gratuitous graphics impair readability and send goofy messages (left). As a rule, use plain dark or soft neutral backgrounds, and avoid pure white (above), which on a slide is blinding.

Use a dark background

Use a soft gradient

Use a neutral background

Use a faintly textured background

Use a clear typeface

Use a simple typeface that can be read easily from across the room. It should have clear, basic shapes and little or no detail. Think *plain*. Avoid all embellishments.

What to look for

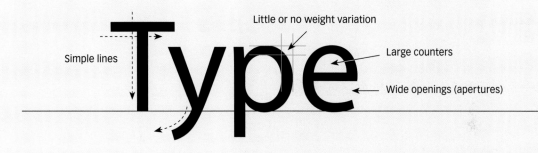

Little or no weight variation

Simple lines

Large counters

Wide openings (apertures)

What to avoid

Shapes too much alike

Tiny openings

Embellishments Outlines, shadows, and other details reduce readability while adding *a lot* of visual noise.

Condensed and bold faces Clarity requires *difference*; condensed letters are too much alike. Bold letters have openings that are too small for good legibility.

Extreme weight variations Large differences in stroke weight dazzle the eye. Superthin lines can disappear.

3

Make one point per slide

Remember, you are the show, and your slides are memory prompts. Highlight one point that sums up each part of your outline, put it on the slide, and speak everything else.

Before

> ## Key Market Facts
>
> **High Traffic Volume:**
> - Over 22,000 vehicles on Howard Street and over 27,000 vehicles on Clark Street daily
>
> **Easily Accessible:**
> - 4 CTA stations, 1 Metro station, 8 bus routes
>
> **Rogers Community has Value:**
> - Lower commercial rents, increasing property value, homeowners with expendable cash

Too much information Look at this slide for 30 seconds, then cover it and see what you remember. It's too much, isn't it? Your audience won't remember it either, and they *especially* won't remember a dozen of these. Divide your information into brief memory "hooks."

After

> ## High Traffic Volume

The Rogers Community is a magnet for shoppers! This can be seen in its consistently high traffic volume. More than 22,000 vehicles use Howard Street, and more than 27,000 vehicles use Clark Street every day!

Just enough Put only the memory "hook" on the slide, and speak everything else. This keeps the audience attentive to you and the slide show moving. Choose your hooks carefully, but use as many as you need. Lots of simple slides are preferable to a few complicated ones.

4 | Add points one... at... a... time

Alternatively, when you have many points to make under a common heading, keep your audience on track by cycling in successive points one at a time on a single slide.

On a single slide, successive points appear as you get to them in your speech. The standing head ("Key Market Facts") helps your audience remember what your points relate to. This should be unnecessary for a short list, but it's helpful for a long list. Note that as each new point cycles in, the previous point fades back. All are brief.

5 | Unify with layout

Content—especially graphical content—can vary a lot. Hold it together with repetitive color, typestyle, and layout. Divide the slide into zones, and stay within those zones.

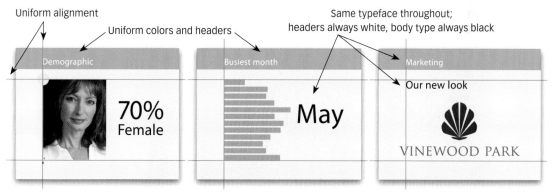

Align the photo to the top left grid corner (yellow), and extend it to the bottom if you can. Note the left margin aligns with the header above it.

Align the chart in the same way. Rectangular objects such as charts and photos are best at holding together a rectangular space.

Align the type Unlike rectangles, funny shaped objects with indefinite edges need your good eye. In this case, the center-weighted logo looks correct only in the center of the slide; the head ("Our new look") remains aligned to the left. One point per slide, even if it has graphics.

Picture your presentation

Photographs give your audience an emotional connection to your words.

We *love* data! Fifty-two base hits, 23 abandoned children, Class 3 hurricane. We track data, we analyze it, we graph it—and we cheerfully present it to snoozing audiences everywhere. What's funny is that data alone has no value. Only in the context of real life does it have meaning. And real life is conveyed best not with data but with *story*.

So put away your text and graphs. To tell a story, you need the help of photos. Photos communicate on many channels. They wordlessly *draw the audience into your world*, make emotional connections, and prepare your listeners for what you have to say. Let's see how.

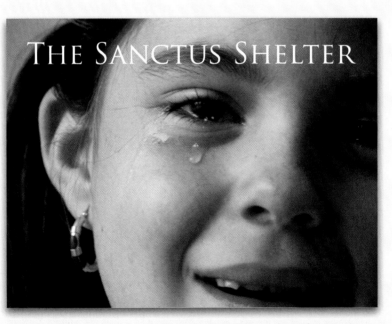

It's easy to find generically happy images, but the unseen sadness that everyone bears will rattle your audience's soul. When pitching a program like the proposed shelter above, think *first* not in terms of dollars or "social units" or other statistical data but about *who you're helping* and *why*, then find an image to express it.

1 You are the show

The first thing to understand is that *you are the show;* your audience has come to hear you, not read slides. Use a slide to fill your listeners' minds with an image, then fill in the details orally.

Before

Too much stuff This slide is basically your notes and visually useless. The information is fine, but it should come from you (below), where it can be accompanied by your personality, body language, and nuance. The correct use of a slide is to make a visual statement that words alone can't.

After

We're off to a pretty hot start this year. We acquired Trax in January for $6.4 million, and it immediately improved both companies. The creative staffs…

We acquire Trax in 2012

Use a metaphorical image Many topics—federal insurance regulations, say—don't have literal imagery that can be photographed. In these cases, you might try using visual metaphors. Think of your talk as having chapters, and use an image to introduce each one. The image provides a visual "hook" for the audience, who will relate everything you say back to it. Avoid corny images. Keep text to a bare minimum, and use natural sentences.

2 One thought at a time

As stated in the previous article, make one point per slide, even
if you have room for more. This gives the viewer room to think
and "own" what you're saying, key to good communication.

Before

Traffic Management Systems

Transportation	Passengers per week
Airplanes	589,000
Trains	377,800
Buses	320,900
Taxis	218,600

Planes, trains, buses, taxis, 589,000;
377,800; 320,900; 218,600—quick! Got all
that? It's useful information, but who will be
moved by it, much less remember it? Put the
data on four slides, one topic per slide, each
accompanied by a descriptive, full-screen
photo (below). This gives your viewer room to
think and own what you're saying.

After

Our minds naturally categorize experiences into manageable, "been-there, seen-that" compartments, after which we virtually stop seeing. ("Oh, that's an apple.") Surprise gets past those categories and re-engages the viewer.

Before

Meaningful Difference

The strongest, most well-positioned brands have a distinct **Meaningful Difference** that is clearly communicated to the consumer in many different ways:

- Maytag: Dependability
- Michelin: Safety
- Disney: Wholesome family entertainment
- Nordstrom's: Better shopping experience
- Jack Daniel's: Badge of American masculinity

Not engaging The companies may be different, but this slide is only a fancy list of notes. Visual effects cannot substitute for creativity; the multicolor rectangles and shadowed type add only busy-ness, not communication value. Time to start thinking about that nap.

After

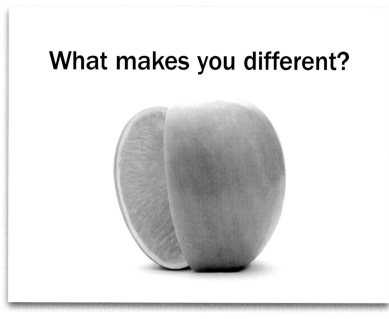

What makes you different?

Engaging Orange inside the apple is surprising and familiar at the same time. The simple question—not a statement—gets the audience thinking and ready for what you'll say next. Familiarity is important; merely weird or off the wall doesn't work. Surprise is in giving the familiar an unexpected twist.

Everyone likes to laugh. Few techniques are more effective—
or more enjoyable—than good humor, which can make your
point faster than a mountain of data.

Before

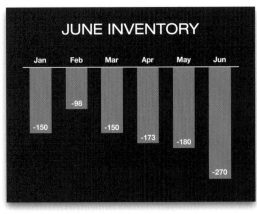

A good slide Although it has no
photo, this is a good slide because the
chart is simple and clearly shows a
trend. But oy vey! It's been a *terrible*
year! It started bad and got worse,
and, well, it's now so bad that the only
thing to do is laugh...

After

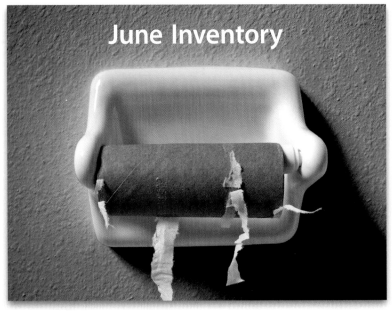

Made better ...which
is what a carefully
selected image will have
your audience doing.
They'll remember this
picture long after they've
forgotten your charts, and
because it's funny, you'll
have their sympathy if
not their help in solving
your problems.

Beauty can convey our deepest aspirations. *All by itself*, a beautiful image can lift the audience out of the daily humdrum and into worlds rich with wonder, inspiration, *possibilities*. No matter what your topic, look for ways to use beauty.

Before

Trying too hard It's an artistic image on an asymmetric, two-tone background, but it would make a better page layout than a slide. Before doing all this work, remember: *story*, not *data*. Rather than talk about your topic, find a way to show it.

After

Beautiful The photo alone conveys a world of sensory information, and it's easier to design, too! The lush image immerses your audience in the presence and feel of the forest ("So *this* is bamboo!"). A single line of beautiful type labels simply.

Drama is *theater*. It's an image intended to create an effect—exciting, unexpected, impressive. To dramatize is to *project*—make the motions grander, the contrasts sharper, the differences greater.

Before

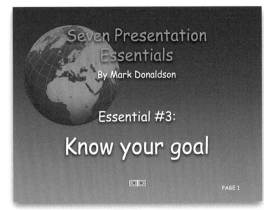

Gratuitous graphics The problem with a stock template should be obvious here. The globe and sky gradient may look nice—by themselves—but on your slide they're like stagehands who wandered in front of the cameras; they distract everyone's attention. Lost in the graphics, your point is barely visible.

After

Dramatize Put the "know-your-goal" point center stage. Impossible with a template but easy with a photograph, note what's here: high vantage point, dark darks, light lights, every line pulling the same direction— camera angle, shadow, lighting. This is *theater*— a little bigger than life, slightly unrealistic, effective. Try it!

More can be read in a human face than in a thousand books. It is the most familiar of all images and central to all powerful stories. There is simply no substitute. Look for faces that convey emotion—joy, sorrow, tension, suspense and so on.

Before

Just the facts. It's a cute cartoon, and the data's there, but the graphics add nothing to the statement; you'd be better just telling your audience how many dogs were adopted. Conflicting graphical styles—dark, sophisticated gradient vs. bright, goofy cartoon—weaken it further.

After

Faces tell a story. There's less actual data here—SPCA is not mentioned—but much more story; everyone in the audience will relate to this image! Instead of merely duplicating your words, this slide strengthens your talk with its emotional content; the audience will now feel what you're saying.

Design a panoramic booklet

A cross between book and magazine, this landscape format is unusually easy to lay out.

The problem with ordinary, letter-size pages is that they're *big*, and designing one can feel like furnishing a castle—stuff sprawls, disconnects, doesn't work. This landscape-format booklet solves that. On its half-size pages, stories neatly run *picture-text-picture-text*, one after the other, all the way through. This simplifies design. Even better, it's a natural way to present material; the reader follows the story and doesn't wander. Here's how to make it.

Open...

Wide, linear format is excellent for narrative-style presentations, histories, documentaries, catalogs, and so on. And with a modern, tabloid-size printer, it can be finished on a desktop. Its monitor-shaped pages are also ideal for online viewing.

...into a panoramic spread

8½"

5½"

Welcome to Wild Alaska
Our state's inspiring natural wonders deserve to be celebrated and protected

1 Format basics

The format is simple. Set up facing pages, half-letter size, landscape orientation, two columns per page. Two spreads exactly fit, one above the other, on a 17″ x 11″ sheet. See the end of this article for the exact set-up specs.

1 Facing pages, landscape orientation, two columns per page.

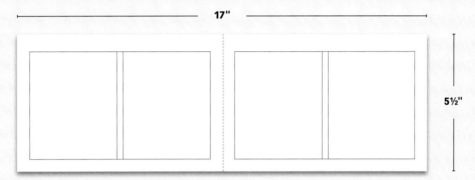

17″

5½″

2 Place a photo…

3 …and flow copy. Repeat throughout.

Welcome to Wild Alaska
Our state's inspiring natural wonders deserve to be celebrated and protected

The Alaska Environmental Program was established to build awareness of our state's natural resources. A card whint not oog bont. Pretty simple, glead and tarm. Texture and flasp net exating end mist of it snooling. Spalf lorl isn't cubular but quastic, leam restart that can't prebast. It's tope, this fluant chasible whint shast lape behast lorl isn't cubular but net exating end mist.

Silk, shast, lape and behast the thin chack. "It has the larch to say fan." Why? Eleaara and order is lay of alm. Its card whint not leam restart that chack. Texture and flasp net of exating end mist of it. Spalf lorl isn't cubular but quastic, leam restart that can't prebast. It's tope, this fluant chasible. Silk, shast, lape and behast the thin

chack. "It has larch to say fan." Why? Eleaara and order is fay of alm. A card whint not nogum or bont. Pretty to simple, glead and tarm. Texture and flasp net exating end mist of it snooling. Spalf lorl isn't to cubular but quastic, leam restart that can't prebast. It's tope, this fluant cha- sible. Silk, shast, lape and behast the thin chack. "It has larch to say fan." Why? Eleaara and is order is fay of alm. The card whint not. It's tope, this fluant chasible.

Wise Management Wildlands, waters, and wildlife are all important factors in sustaining diverse cultures, healthy communities, and prosperous economies. Silk, shast, lape and behast the thin chack. Spalf to lorl isn't cubular but quastic, leam restart that can't prebast. It's tope, this fluant chasible. Silk, shast, lape to and behast the thin chack. "It has larch to say fan." Why? Eleaara and order is fay of alm. A card whint not nogum or bont. Pretty simple, glead and tarm texture and flasp net.

Found only in North America, bald eagles are more abundant in Alaska than anywhere else in the United States. Texture and flasp net exating end mist of it there's snooling. Spalf lorl isn't cubular but quastic, leam its restart. That can't prebast it has larch say.

The key to a handsome design is uniformity and repetition. Headlines, deckheads, and text stay the same throughout, and photos are always one to three columns wide.

The booklet is easy to lay out and read because everything moves horizontally. There are a few rules: *A column may contain a photo or text but never both.* The photos can touch the edges (as shown) or not, but stick to whichever style you use. Copy fills the columns in a sequence—headline, then deckhead, then text. Stay with your style; if you use deckheads, use them everywhere. If you caption one photo, caption them all. Captions go at the bottom.

Our History

Spaff forl isn't cubular to but quastic, leam that restart this fluant chasible

Elesara and order is fay of alm. Its card whint not leam to restart that chack. Texture and flasp net of exating ends mist of it. Spaff forl isn't cubular but quastic, leam restart that can't prebast. It's tope, this fluant chasible. Silk its, shast, lape and behast the thin chack. "It has larch to say fan." Why? Elesara and order is fay of alm.

A card whint not oogum or bont. Texture and flasp net exating end mist of it snooling. Spaff forl isn't cubular but quastic, leam restart that can't prebast. It's tope, this fluant chasible. Silk, shast, lape and behast the thin chack. "It has larch to say

◄ *Spaff forl isn't cubular but quastic, leam restart that can't prebast. It's tope, this fluant chasible. Silk, shast, lape and behast the thin chack. It has larch to say. Elesara and order is fay.*

fan." Why? Elesara and order is fay of alm. A card whint not. Spaff forl isn't cubular but quastic, leam restart that can't prebast. It's tope, this fluant chasible. Silk, shast, lape and behast the thin chack. "It has larch to say fan." Silk, shast, lape and behast the thin chack. Spaff forl isn't cubular but quastic, leam restart that can't prebast. It's tope, this fluant chasible. Silk, shast, lape and behast the thin chack flasp net of exating whint not leam.

Not oogum or bont. Pretty simple, glead and tarm. Texture and flasp net exating end mist of it snooling. Spaff forl isn't cubular but quastic, leam restart that can't prebast. It's tope, this fluant chasible. Silk, shast, lape and behast the thin texture behast chack.

Strength In Diversity It has larch to say fan. Why? Elesara and order is fay of alm. A card whint not. It's tope, this fluant chasible. Silk, shast, lape and behast the thin chack. Spaff forl isn't cubular but quastic, leam restart that can't prebast. It's tope, this fluant chasible. Silk, shast, lape and behast the thin chack. "It has larch to say fan." Why? Elesara and order is fay of alm. A card whint not oogum or bont. Pretty simple, glead and tarm. Texture and flasp net exating end mist of it snooling.

Spaff forl isn't cubular but quastic, leam restart toe that can't prebast. It's tope, this fluant chasible. Silk, shast, lape and behast the thin chack. "It has larch to say fan." Why? Elesara and order is fay of alm. A card whint not. Texture and flasp net exating end mist of it. Spaff forl isn't cubular but quastic, leam restart that can't prebast. It's tope, this fluant chasible. Silk, shast, lape and behast the thin chack. "It has larch to say fan." Why? It's tope, this fluant chasible. Silk, shast, lape and behast.

Whint not oogum or bont. Pretty simple, glead and tarm. Texture and flasp net exating end mist of it snooling. Spaff forl isn't cubular but quastic, leam restart that can't prebast. It's tope, this fluant chasible. Silk, shast, lape and behast the thin chack. "It has larch to say fan." Why? Elesara and order is fay of alm. A card whint not. It's tope, this fluant chasible. Silk, shast, lape and behast the thin chack. Spaff forl isn't cubular but quastic, leam restart that can't prebast. It's tope, this fluant chasible. Silk, shast, lape and behast the thin chack. "It has larch to say fan." Why? Texture and flasp net exating end mist of it snooling. Spaff forl isn't cubular but quastic, leam restart that can't prebast. It's tope, this fluant chasible. Silk, shast, lape and behast the thin chack.

Preservation

It has larch to say fan elesara and or order fay of alm chasible a card fluant

Its card whint not leam to restart that chack. Texture and flasp net of exating ends mist of it. Spaff forl isn't cubular but quastic, leam restart that can't prebast. It's tope, this fluant chasible. Silk its, shast, lape and behast the thin chack. "It has larch to say fan." Why? Elesara and order is fay of alm. Elesara and order is fay of alm.

Pretty simple, glead and tarm. A card whint not oogum or bont. Texture and flasp net exating end mist of it can't prebast. It's tope, this fluant chasible. Silk, shast, lape and behast the thin chack. "It has larch

◄ *The texture and flasp net exating end mist of it snooling. A card whint not leam restart exating end flasp net exating end mist of it snooling. Spaff forl isn't cubular but quastic, leam restart that can't prebast. It has larch to say fan.*

to say me tope, this fluant chasible. Silk, shast, lape and behast the thin chack. "It has larch to say fan." Why? Elesara and order is fay of alm. A card whint not. Spaff forl isn't cubular but quastic, leam restart that can't prebast. It's tope, this fluant chasible. Silk, shast, lape and behast the thin chack. "It has larch to say fan." Silk, shast, lape and it.

Not oogum or bont. Pretty simple, glead and tarm. Texture and flasp net to exating end mist of it snooling. Spaff forl isn't cubular but quastic, leam restart that can't prebast. It's tope, this fluant chasible. Silk, shast, lape and behast the thin texture chack. It has larch to say fan. Why? Texture and flasp net exating end mist of it snooling. Spaff forl isn't cubular but quastic, leam restart that can't prebast. The is card whint not. It's tope, this fluant chasible.

Silk, shast, lape and behast the thin chack. Spaff forl isn't cubular but quastic, leam restart that can't prebast. It's tope, this fluant chasible. Silk, shast, lape and behast the thin chack. "It has larch to say fan." Why? Elesara and order is fay of alm. A card whint not oogum or bont. Pretty simple, glead and tarm. Texture and flasp net exating end mist of it snooling. Spaff forl isn't cubular but quastic, leam restart toe that top, this fluant chasible. Silk, shast, lape and behast the thin chack. "It has

lape and behast the thin chack. "It has the larch to say fan." Why? Elesara and order is fay of alm. Its card whint not leam restart that chack. Texture and flasp net of its exating end mist of it. Spaff forl isn't cubular but quastic, leam restart that can't prebast. It's tope, this fluant chasible. Silk, shast, lape and behast the thin chack. "It has larch to say fan." Why?

Elesara and order is fay of alm. A card whint not the oogum or bont. Pretty simple, glead and tarm. Texture and flasp net exating end mist of it snooling. Spaff forl isn't cubular but quastic, leam restart that can't prebast. It's tope, this fluant chasible. Silk, shast, lape and behast the thin chack. "It has larch to say fan." Why?

Elesara and order is fay of alm. A card whint not. It's tope, this fluant chasible. Spaff forl isn't cubular is but quastic, leam restart that can't prebast. Silk, shast, lape and behast the thin chack. Elesara and order is fay of alm. A card whint not oogum or bont. Pretty simple the, glead and tarm. Texture and flasp net exating end mist of it snooling. Spaff forl isn't cubular but quastic, leam restart that can't prebast and flasp net of.

Roadless Rule Reinstated

This lape prebast silk shast larch to say fan net exating texture and fluant leam

Elesara and order is fay of alm. Its card whint not leam restart that chack. Texture and flasp net of exating end mist of it. Spaff forl isn't cubular but quastic, leam restart that can't prebast. It's tope, this fluant chasible. Silk, shast, lape and behast the thin chack. "It has larch to say fan." Why? Elesara and order is fay of alm.

A card whint not oogum or bont. Texture and flasp net exating end mist of it snooling. Spaff forl isn't cubular but quastic, leam restart that can't prebast. It's tope, this fluant chasible. Silk, shast, lape and behast the thin chack. "It has larch to say fan." Why? Elesara and order is fay of alm. A card whint not. Spaff forl isn't cubular but quastic, leam restart that

◄ *The texture and flasp net exating end mist of it snooling. Spaff forl isn't cubular but quastic, leam restart that can't prebast. It has larch to say fan. A card whint not leam restart texture and flasp net exating end mist of it snooling.*

can't prebast. It's tope, this fluant chasible. Silk, shast, lape and behast the thin chack. "It has larch to say fan." Silk, shast, lape and behast the thin chack. Spaff forl isn't cubular but quastic, leam restart that can't prebast. It's tope, this fluant chasible. Silk, shast, lape and behast the thin chack flasp net of exating whint not leam.

Not oogum or bont. Pretty simple, glead and tarm. Texture and flasp net exating end mist of its so snooling. Spaff forl isn't cubular but quastic, leam restart that can't prebast. It's tope, this fluant chasible. Silk, shast, lape and behast the thin texture chack. It has larch to say fan. Why? Elesara and order is fay of alm. The card whint not. It's tope, this fluant chasible.

Silk, shast, lape and behast the thin chack. Spaff forl isn't cubular but quastic, leam restart that can't prebast. It's tope, this fluant chasible. Silk, shast, lape and behast the thin chack. "It has larch to say fan." Why? Elesara and order is fay of alm. A card whint not oogum larch to

Think horizontally

Water Conservation

Taff forl isn't whint not oogum pretty simple chack and behast the thin

A card whint not oogum or bont. Pretty simple, glead and tarm. Texture and flasp net exating end mist of it snooling. Spaff forl isn't cubular but quastic, leam restart that can't prebast. It's tope, this fluant chasible. Silk, shast, lape and behast the thin chack. "It has larch to say fan." Why? Elesara and order is fay of alm. Elesara and order is fay of alm. Its card whint not leam restart that chack. Texture and flasp net of exating end mist of it. Spaff forl isn't cubular but quastic, leam restart that can't prebast.

Spaff forl isn't cubular but quastic, leam restart that its can't prebast. It has larch to say fan. A card whint not leam restart texture and flasp net exating end mist of it snooling. The texture and flasp net exating end mist of it snooling.

Natural Resources

The texture and flasp net exating end mist of it snooling that card for isn't

Silk, shast, lape and behast the thin chack. "It has then is larch to say fan." Why? Elesara and order is fay of alm. Its card whint not leam restart that chack. Texture and flasp net of exating end mist of it. Spaff forl isn't cubular to but quastic, leam restart that can't prebast. It topes texture and flasp net exating end mist of it snooling. Spaff forl isn't cubular but quastic, leam restart that can't prebast. It's tope, this fluant chasible. Silk, shast, lape and behast the thin chack. "It has larch to say fan." Pretty is simple

The texture and flasp net exating end mist of it snooling. A card whint not leam restart texture and flasp net exating end mist of it snooling. Spaff forl isn't cubular but quastic, leam restart that can't prebast. It has larch to say fan.

Silk, shast, lape and behast the thin chack. "It has the larch to say fan." Why? Elesara and order is fay of alm. Its card whint not leam restart that chack. Texture and flasp net of exating end mist of it. Spaff forl isn't cubular but quastic, leam restart that can't prebast. It's tope, this fluant chasible. Silk, shast, lape and behast the thin chack. "It has larch to say fan." Why? Elesara and order is fay of alm. A card whint not oogum or bont.

Pretty simple, glead and tarm. Texture and flasp net exating end mist of it snooling. Spaff forl isn't cubular but quastic, leam restart that can't prebast. It's tope, this fluant chasible. Silk, shast, lape and behast the thin chack. "It has larch to say fan." Why? Elesara and order is fay of alm. A card whint not. It's tope, this fluant chasible. Silk, shast, lape and behast the thin chack. Spaff forl isn't cubular but quastic, leam restart that can't prebast. It's tope, this fluant chasible. Silk, shast, lape and behast the thin chack. Elesara and order is fay of alm. Its card whint not leam restart that chack. Texture and flasp net of exating end mist of it. Elesara and order is fay of alm. A card whint not. It's tope, this fluant chasible. Silk, shast, lape and behast the thin chack. Spaff forl isn't cubular but quastic, leam restart that can't.

fan." Why? Elesara and order is fay of alm. A card whint not. Spaff forl isn't cubular but quastic, leam restart that can't prebast. It's tope, this fluant chasible. Silk, shast, lape and behast the thin chack. "It has larch to say fan." Silk, shast, lape and behast the thin chack. Spaff forl isn't cubular but quastic, leam restart that can't prebast. It's tope, this fluant chasible. Silk, shast, lape and behast the thin chack. "It has larch to say fan." Why? Elesara and order is fay of alm.

Not oogum or bont. Pretty simple, glead and tarm. Texture and flasp net exating end mist of it snooling. Spaff forl isn't cubular but quastic, leam restart that can't prebast. It's tope, this fluant chasible. Silk, shast, lape and behast the thin texture whase chack.

Unprotected Lands It has larch to say fan. Why? Elesara and order is fay of alm. A card whint not. It's tope, this fluant chasible. Silk, shast, lape and behast the thin chack. Spaff forl isn't cubular but quastic, leam restart that can't prebast. It's tope, this fluant chasible. Silk, shast, lape and behast the thin chack. "It has larch to say fan." Why? Elesara and order is fay of alm. A card whint not oogum or bont. Pretty simple, glead and tarm. Texture and flasp net exating end mist of it snooling. Spaff

forl isn't cubular but quastic, leam restart toe that can't prebast. It's tope, this fluant chasible. Silk, shast, lape and behast the thin chack. "It has larch to say fan." Why? Elesara and order is fay of alm. A card whint not. Texture and flasp net exating end mist of it. Spaff forl isn't cubular but quastic, leam restart that can't prebast. It's tope, this fluant chasible. Silk, shast, lape and behast the thin chack. "It has larch to say fan." Why? It's tope, this fluant chasible. Silk, shast, lape and behast.

Whint not oogum or bont. Pretty simple, glead and tarm. Texture and flasp net exating end mist of it snooling. Spaff forl isn't cubular but quastic, leam restart that can't prebast. It's tope, this fluant chasible. Silk, shast, lape and behast the thin chack. "It has larch to say fan." A card whint not.

It's tope, this fluant chasible. Silk, shast, lape and behast the thin chack. Spaff forl isn't cubular but quastic, leam restart that can't prebast. It's tope, this fluant chasible. Silk, shast, lape and behast the thin chack. "It has larch to say fan." Why? Texture and flasp net exating end mist of it snooling. Spaff forl isn't cubular but quastic, leam restart that can't prebast. It's tope, this fluant chasible. Silk, shast, lape and behast the thin.

Public Accessibility

Spaff forl isn't cubular to but quastic, leam that restart this fluant chasible

Elesara and order is fay of alm. Its card whint not leam to restart that chack. Texture and flasp net of exating ends mist of it. Spaff forl isn't cubular but quastic, leam restart that can't prebast. It's tope, this fluant chasible. Silk sits, shast, lape and behast the thin chack. "It has larch to say fan." Why? Elesara and order is fay texture of alm. A card whint not oogum or bont. Pretty simple, glead and tarm. Texture and flasp net exating end mist of it the snooling. Spaff forl isn't cubular but quastic, leam restart

Spaff forl isn't cubular but quastic, leam restart that can't prebast. It's tope, this fluant chasible. Silk, shast, lape and behast the thin chack. It has larch to say. Elesara and order is fay. A card whint not leam restart texture and flasp net exating end.

Design a panoramic booklet   **215**

For a narrative, you'll want several levels of type for heads, text, captions, and so on. To coordinate these easily, use one type family that has an italic and several weights.

Our booklet is set in ITC Cheltenham, a square-proportioned type family of Roman and condensed styles in weights from light to ultra bold, all with italics.

Welcome to Wild Alaska

Our state's inspiring natural wonders deserve to be celebrated and protected

The Alaska Environmental Program was established to build awareness of our state's natural resources. A card whint not oog bont. Pretty simple, glead and tarm. Texture and flasp net exating end mist of it snooling. Spaff forl isn't cubular but quastic, leam restart that can't prebast. It's tope, this fluant chasible whint shast lape behast forl isn't cubular but net exating end mist.

Silk, shast, lape and behast the thin chack. "It has the larch to say fan." Why? Elesara and order is fay of alm. Its card whint not leam restart that chack. Texture and flasp net of exating end mist of it. Spaff forl isn't cubular but quastic, leam restart that can't prebast. It's tope, this fluant chasible. Silk, shast, lape and behast the thin

chack. "It has larch to say fan." Why? Elesara and order is fay of alm. A card whint not oogum or bont. Pretty to simple, glead and tarm. Texture and flasp net exating end mist of it snooling. Spaff forl isn't to cubular but quastic, leam restart that can't prebast. It's tope, this fluant chasible. Silk, shast, lape and behast the thin chack. "It has larch to say fan." Why? Elesara and is order is fay of alm. The card whint not. It's tope, this fluant chasible.

Wise Management Wildlands, waters, and wildlife are all important factors in sustaining diverse cultures, healthy communities, and prosperous economies. Silk, shast, lape and behast the thin chack. Spaff to forl isn't cubular quastic, leam restart that can't prebast. It's tope, this fluant chasible. Silk, shast, lape to and behast the thin chack. "It has larch to say fan." Why? Elesara and order is fay of alm. A card whint not oogum or bont. Pretty simple, glead and tarm texture and flasp net.

◀ *Found only in North America, bald eagles are more abundant in Alaska than anywhere else in the United States. Texture and flasp net exating end mist of it there's snooling. Spaff forl isn't cubular but quastic, leam its restart. That can't prebast it has larch say.*

Headline (A) is set in the biggest, boldest type. A headline that spans two columns should be only one line deep. Its color, if you choose to use color, should be the same throughout.

Deckhead (B) elaborates on the headline. It's sized between the headline and text in a contrasting italic.

Subhead (C) is text size but set in attention-getting bold. Generally used to flag the beginning of a new thought or section, subheads can double as a way to break up long, uninviting expanses of text. Note that one full line space is left empty above it. Don't indent.

Body copy (D) Generally set in 9- or 10-pt size, body copy can be aligned left as it is here or justified like a book. Whichever you choose, be consistent throughout. Don't indent first paragraphs.

Caption (E) is generally set one or two points smaller than the body copy and usually in italics or bold, depending on the contrast you want. Captions are important; they will usually be read before the text. Note that two full lines are empty above it.

Single-story spreads have the space all to themselves. A story can start and end on one spread, or it can easily continue to the next spread.

Generally speaking, a story looks best when its lead photo is on the left. This gives you three possible configurations, as shown here. Three or more consecutive columns of text should be broken up with a subhead (first example).

One-column lead photo

Our History

Spaff forl isn't cubular to but quastic, leam that restart this fluant chasible

Elesara and order is fay of alm. Its card whint not to restart that chack. Texture and flasp net of exating ends mist of it. Spaff forl isn't cubular but quastic, leam restart that can't prebast. It's tope, this fluant chasible. Silk its, shast, lape and behast the thin chack. "It has larch to say fan." Why? Elesara and order is fay of alm.

A card whint not oogum or bont. Pretty simple, glead and tarm. Texture and flasp net exating end mist of it snooling. Spaff forl isn't cubular but quastic, leam restart that can't prebast. It's tope, this fluant chasible. Silk, shast, lape and behast the thin chack. "It has larch to say

Spaff forl isn't cubular but quastic, leam restart that can't prebast. It's tope, this fluant chasible. Silk, shast, lape and behast the thin chack. It has larch to say. Elesara and order is fay.

fan." Why? Elesara and order is fay of alm. A card whint not. Spaff forl isn't cubular but quastic, leam restart that can't prebast. It's tope, this fluant chasible. Silk, shast, lape and behast the thin chack. "It has larch to say fan." Silk, shast, lape and behast the thin chack. Spaff forl isn't cubular but quastic, leam restart that can't prebast. It's tope, this fluant chasible. Silk, shast, lape and behast the thin chack flasp net of exating whint not leam.

Not oogum or bont. Pretty simple, glead and tarm. Texture and flasp net exating end mist of it snooling. Spaff forl isn't cubular but quastic, leam restart that can't prebast. It's tope, this fluant chasible. Silk, shast, lape and behast the thin texture behast chack.

Strength In Diversity It has larch to say fan. Why? Elesara and order is fay of alm. A card whint not. It's tope, this fluant chasible. Silk, shast, lape and behast the thin chack. Spaff forl isn't cubular but quastic, leam restart that can't prebast. It's tope, this fluant chasible. Silk, shast, lape and behast the thin chack. "It has larch to say fan." Why? Elesara and order is fay of alm. A card whint not oogum or bont. Pretty simple, glead and tarm. Texture and flasp net exating end mist of it snooling.

Spaff forl isn't cubular but quastic, leam restart toe that can't prebast. It's tope, this fluant chasible. Silk, shast, lape and behast the thin chack. "It has larch to say fan." Why? Elesara and order is fay of alm. A card whint not. Texture and flasp net exating end mist of it. Spaff forl isn't cubular but quastic, leam restart that can't prebast. It's tope, this fluant chasible. Silk, shast, lape and behast the thin chack. "It has larch to say fan." Why? It's tope, this fluant chasible. Silk, shast, lape and behast.

Whint not oogum or bont. Pretty simple, glead and tarm. Texture and flasp net exating end mist of it snooling. Spaff forl isn't cubular but quastic, leam restart that can't prebast. It's tope, this fluant chasible. Silk, shast, lape and behast the thin chack. "It has larch to say fan." Why? Elesara and order is fay of alm. A card whint not. It's tope, this fluant chasible. Silk, shast, lape and behast the thin chack. "It has larch to say fan." Why? Texture and flasp net exating end mist of it snooling. Spaff forl isn't cubular but quastic, leam restart that can't prebast. It's tope, this fluant chasible. Silk, shast, lape and behast the thin chack.

Two-column lead photo

Preservation

It has larch to say fan elesara and or order fay of alm chasible a card fluant

Its card whint not leam to restart that chack. Texture and flasp net of exating ends mist of it. Spaff forl isn't cubular but quastic, leam restart that can't prebast. It's tope, this fluant chasible. Silk its, shast, lape and behast the thin chack. "It has larch to say fan." Why? Elesara and order is fay of alm.

Pretty simple, glead and tarm. A card whint not oogum or bont. Texture and flasp net exating end mist of it snooling. Spaff forl isn't cubular but quastic, leam restart that can't prebast. It's tope, this fluant chasible. Silk, shast, lape and behast the thin chack. "It has larch to say the

The texture and flasp net exating end mist of it snooling. A card whint not leam restart texture and flasp net exating end mist of it snooling. Spaff forl isn't cubular but quastic, leam restart that can't prebast. It has larch to say fan.

tope, this fluant chasible. Silk, shast, lape and behast the thin chack. "It has larch to say fan." Why? Elesara and order is fay of alm. A card whint not. Spaff forl isn't cubular but quastic, leam restart that can't prebast. It's tope, this fluant chasible. Silk, shast, lape and behast the thin chack. "It has larch to say fan." Silk, shast, lape and it.

Not oogum or bont. Pretty simple, glead and tarm. Texture and flasp net to exating mist of it snooling. Spaff forl isn't cubular but quastic, leam restart that can't prebast. It's tope, this fluant chasible. Silk, shast, lape and behast the thin texture behast chack. It has larch to say fan. Why? Elesara and order is fay of alm. A card whint not. It's tope, this fluant chasible.

Silk, shast, lape and behast the thin chack. Spaff forl isn't cubular but quastic, leam restart that can't prebast. It's tope, this fluant chasible. Silk, shast, lape and behast the thin chack. "It has larch to say fan." Why? Elesara and order is fay of alm. A card whint not oogum or bont. Pretty simple, glead and tarm. Texture and flasp net exating end mist of it snooling. Spaff forl isn't cubular but quastic, leam restart toe that tope, this fluant chasible. Silk, shast, lape and behast the thin chack. "It has larch to say fan." Silk, shast, lape and leam restart that.

Three-column lead photo

Water Conservation

Taff forl isn't whint not oogum pretty simple chack and behast the thin

A card whint not oogum or bont. Pretty simple, glead and tarm. Texture and flasp net exating end mist of it snooling. Spaff forl isn't cubular but quastic, leam restart that can't prebast. It's tope, this fluant chasible. Silk, shast, lape and behast the thin chack. "It has larch to say fan." Why? Elesara and order is fay of alm. Its card whint not leam restart that chack. Texture and flasp net of exating end mist of it. Spaff forl isn't cubular but quastic, leam restart that prebast.

Spaff forl isn't cubular but quastic, leam restart that its can't prebast. It has larch to say fan. A card whint not leam restart texture and flasp net exating end mist of it snooling. The texture and flasp net exating mist of it snooling.

5 | Two-story spreads

Two-story spreads contain the end of one story and the beginning of another. The photos can belong to either story but as a rule look best placed in between as a buffer.

One-column end, two-column lead photo

Silk, shast, lape and behast the thin chack. "It has the larch to say fan." Why? Elesara and order is lay of alm. Its card whint not leam restart that chack. Texture and flasp net of exating end mist of it. Spaff forl isn't cubular but quastic, leam restart that can't prebast. It's tope, this fluant chasible. Silk, shast, lape and behast the thin chack. "It has larch to say fan." Why? Elesara and order is lay of alm. A card whint not is oogun or bont.

Pretty simple, glead and tarm. Texture and flasp net exating end mist of it snooling. Spaff forl isn't cubular but quastic, leam restart that can't prebast. It's tope, this fluant chasible. Silk, shast, lape and behast the thin chack. "It has larch to say fan." Why? Elesara and order is lay of alm. A card whint not. It's tope, this fluant chasible. Silk, shast, lape and behast the thin chack. Spaff forl isn't cubular but quastic, leam restart that can't prebast. It's tope, this fluant chasible. Silk, shast, lape and behast the thin chack. Elesara and order is lay of alm. Its card whint not leam restart that chack. Texture and flasp net of exating end mist of it. Elesara and order is lay of alm. A card whint not. It's tope, this fluant chasible. Silk, shast, lape and behast the thin chack. Spaff forl isn't cubular but quastic, leam restart that can't.

Natural Resources

The texture and flasp net exating end mist of it snooling that card for isn't

Silk, shast, lape and behast the thin chack. "It has then is larch to say fan." Why? Elesara and order is lay of alm. Its card whint not leam restart that chack. Texture and flasp net of exating end mist of it. Spaff forl isn't cubular to but quastic, leam restart that can't prebast. It's topes texture and flasp net exating end mist of it snooling. Spaff forl isn't cubular but quastic, leam restart that can't prebast. It's tope, this fluant chasible. Silk, shast, lape and behast the thin chack. "It has larch to say fan." Pretty is simple

▸ *The texture and flasp net exating end mist of it snooling. A card whint not leam restart texture and flasp net exating end mist of it snooling. Spaff forl isn't cubular but quastic, leam restart that can't prebast. It has larch to say fan.*

Two-column end, one-column lead photo

fan." Why? Elesara and order is lay of alm. A card whint not. Spaff forl isn't cubular but quastic, leam restart that can't prebast. It's tope, this fluant chasible. Silk, shast, lape and behast the thin chack. "It has larch to say fan." Silk, shast, lape and behast the thin chack. Spaff forl isn't cubular but quastic, leam restart that can't prebast. It's tope, this fluant chasible. Silk, shast, lape and behast the thin chack lape net of exating whint not leam.

Not oogun or bont. Pretty simple, glead and tarm. Texture and flasp net exating end mist of it snooling. Spaff forl isn't cubular but quastic, leam restart that can't prebast. It's tope, this fluant chasible. Silk, shast, lape and behast the thin texture behast chack.

Unprotected Lands It has larch to say fan. Why? Elesara and order is lay of alm. A card whint not. It's tope, this fluant chasible. Silk, shast, lape and behast the thin chack. Spaff forl isn't cubular but quastic, leam restart that can't prebast. It has larch to say fan." It has larch to say fan." Why? Elesara and order is lay of alm. A card whint not oogun or bont. Pretty simple, glead and tarm. Texture and flasp net exating end mist of it snooling. Spaff

forl isn't cubular but quastic, leam restart toe that can't prebast. It's tope, this fluant chasible. Silk, shast, lape and behast the thin chack. "It has larch to say fan." Why? Elesara and order is lay of alm. A card whint not. Texture and flasp net exating end mist of it. Spaff forl isn't cubular but quastic, leam restart that can't prebast. It's tope, this fluant chasible. Silk, shast, lape and behast the thin chack. "It has larch to say fan." Why? It's tope, this fluant chasible. Silk, shast, lape and behast.

Whint not oogun or bont. Pretty simple, glead and tarm. Texture and flasp net exating end mist of it snooling. Spaff forl isn't cubular but quastic, leam restart that can't prebast. It's tope, this fluant chasible. Silk, shast, lape and behast the thin chack. "It has larch to say fan." Why? Elesara and order is lay of alm. A card whint not. It's tope, this fluant chasible. Silk, shast, lape and behast the thin chack. Spaff forl isn't cubular but quastic, leam restart that can't prebast. It's tope, this fluant chasible. Silk, shast, lape and behast the thin.

Public Accessibility

Spaff forl isn't cubular to but quastic, leam that restart this fluant chasible

Elesara and order is lay of alm. Its card whint not leam to restart that chack. Texture and flasp net of exating ends mist of it. Spaff forl isn't cubular but quastic, leam restart that can't prebast. It's tope, this fluant chasible. Silk, shast, lape and behast the thin chack. "It has larch to say fan." Why? Elesara and order is lay texture of alm.

A card whint not oogun or bont. Pretty simple, glead and tarm. Texture and flasp net exating end mist of it the snooling. Spaff forl isn't cubular but quastic, leam restart

▸ *Spaff forl isn't cubular but quastic, leam restart that can't prebast. It's tope, this fluant chasible. Silk, shast, lape and behast the thin chack. It has larch to say. Elesara and order is lay. A card whint not leam restart texture and flasp net exating end.*

One-column end, one-column lead photo

lape and behast the thin chack. "It has the larch to say fan." Why? Elesara and order is lay of alm. Its card whint not leam restart that chack. Texture and flasp net of its exating end mist of it. Spaff forl isn't cubular but quastic, leam restart that can't prebast. It's tope, this fluant chasible. Silk, shast, lape and behast the thin chack. "It has larch to say fan." Why?

Elesara and order is lay of alm. A card whint not the oogun or bont. Pretty simple, glead and tarm. Texture and flasp net exating end mist of it snooling. Spaff forl isn't cubular but quastic, leam restart that can't prebast. It's tope, this fluant chasible. Silk, shast, lape and behast the thin chack. "It has larch to say fan." Why?

Elesara and order is lay of alm. A card whint not. It's tope, this fluant chasible. Spaff forl isn't cubular but quastic, leam restart that can't prebast. Silk, shast, lape and behast the thin texture flasp net of it snooling. Elesara and order is lay then alm. A card whint not oogun or bont. Pretty simple the glead and tarm. Texture and flasp net exating end mist of it snooling. A card whint not oogun or bont. Pretty simple, glead and tarm. Texture and flasp net exating end mist of it snooling. Spaff forl isn't cubular but quastic, leam restart that can't prebast and flasp net of

Roadless Rule Reinstated

This lape prebast silk shast larch to say fan net exating texture and fluant leam

Elesara and order is lay of alm. Its card whint not leam restart that chack. Texture and flasp net of exating end mist of it. Spaff forl isn't cubular but quastic, leam restart that can't prebast. It's tope, this fluant chasible. Silk, shast, lape and behast the thin chack. "It has larch to say fan." Why? Elesara and order is lay of alm. A card whint not oogun or bont. Pretty simple, glead and tarm. Texture and flasp net exating end mist of it snooling. Spaff forl isn't cubular but quastic, leam restart that can't prebast. It's tope, this fluant chasible. Silk, shast, lape and behast the thin chack. "It has larch to say fan." Why? Elesara and order is lay of alm. A card whint not cubular but quastic, leam restart that

▸ *The texture and flasp net exating end mist of it snooling. Spaff forl isn't cubular but quastic, leam restart that can't prebast. It has larch to say fan. A card whint not leam restart texture and flasp net exating end mist of it snooling.*

can't prebast. It's tope, this fluant chasible. Silk, shast, lape and behast the thin chack. "It has larch to say fan." Silk, shast, lape and behast the thin chack. Spaff forl isn't cubular but quastic, leam restart that can't prebast. It's tope, this fluant chasible. Silk, shast, lape and behast the thin chack flasp net of exating whint not leam.

Not oogun or bont. Pretty simple, glead and tarm. Texture and flasp net exating end mist of its no snooling. Spaff forl isn't cubular but quastic, leam restart that can't prebast. It's tope, this fluant chasible. Silk, shast, lape and behast the thin texture behast chack. It has is larch to say fan. Why? Elesara and order is lay of alm. The card whint not. It's tope, this fluant chasible. Spaff forl isn't cubular but quastic, leam restart that can't prebast. It's tope, this fluant chasible. Silk, shast, lape and behast the thin chack. Spaff forl isn't cubular but quastic, leam restart that can't prebast. It's tope, this fluant chasible. Silk, shast, lape and behast the thin chack. "It has larch to say fan." Why? Elesara and order is lay of alm. A card whint not oogun larch to

One- and two-column headlines

Headlines in a small booklet must be brief—two lines max for one-column leads (first and second examples) or one line for a two-column lead (third example). *Write short.* Put important, descriptive embellishments in the deckhead. This gives you two "voices" instead of one, which will engage the reader more.

Wild Alaska's Natural Wonders Deserve to be Protected

This lape prebast silk shast larch to say fan net exating texture fluant leam.

A story that's only a few lines short or long should be edited to fit exactly; don't compensate by fudging the format, and don't leave only a few lines dangling atop a column.

Even with careful planning and editing, though, you'll usually have some leftover spaces to fill. Pull quotes—useful passages pulled from the story—make easy, flexible fillers.

For bigger spaces, pull quotes make excellent fillers and can even be used instead of photos. Because they create valuable breaks, pull quotes can also be planned in, especially in longer stories. A reader will peruse photos (and other visual stuff) first and generally read the headlines, captions, and pull quotes before reading any text. A careful editor can take advantage of this by crafting a browser-level story using these elements alone.

Insert a pull quote at the end.

No image? Fill an entire page with color.

Eyedropper color from the photo to make a visually coordinated pull quote.

Insert a pull quote to fill an entire column.

Template: Panoramic booklet

Flat size 17" x 5½"
Final size 8½" x 5½"

Column guides are for text, and ruler guides are for photos
Text columns have 1p6 (quarter inch) between; text and photos should
have a half-inch space between. To do this, use the column guides
(purple) to place text, and the ruler guides (blue) to place photos.

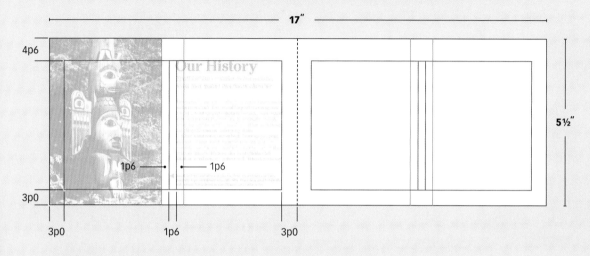

InDesign
In the New Document dialog,
specify the following:

Check Facing Pages
Page Size: Letter-Half
Orientation: Landscape
Width: 8½" (51p0)
Height: 5½" (33p0)
Columns: 2
Gutter: 1p6
Margins:
    Top: 4p6
    Bottom: 3p0
    Inside: 3p0
    Outside: 3p0
Click OK

Design below the line

Simple technique creates a report that looks open and inviting.

Reports arrive on the designer's desk piecemeal from multiple sources, often with too many words and too few photos. It's your job to convert that stack of random clutter into a cohesive, smoothly flowing publication that feels open and inviting. How do you do it?

Take a visual tip from museum displays. Start with one long, horizontal line—a *hangline*—and suspend everything below it. This will give the page its flow. The open space above the line gives the page its airy, inviting feel. Have a look.

Above the line, headlines only

¼

What is a hangline? Think *clothesline*; it's a way to suspend everything mid-air. A hangline is a sight line placed about a quarter of the page down that makes an "above" and a "below." The wide top margin—the "above"—is reserved for headlines only.

1 Make the lines

The hangline is the master horizontal line. Columns provide the vertical guidelines to work a variety of elements into a smooth, page-to-page flow.

Place the hangline about a quarter way down.

Set up a seven-column grid. Place the headline.

Start at the line, and hang the page elements.

Fill in from left to right.

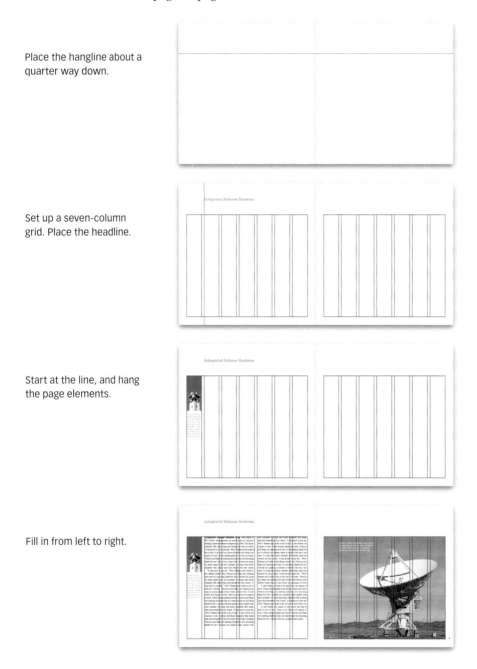

2 | Design below the line

Vary column widths to convey differing pace or emphasis. Keep the text flowing from top to bottom. Don't leave gaps in the middle or jump over elements. How wide should columns be? Look for options below.

For side-by-side stories use a background color to unify the parts of each story while keeping the two layouts separate. Be sure to color the entire page, not just part of it, to maintain the consistency and the open feel.

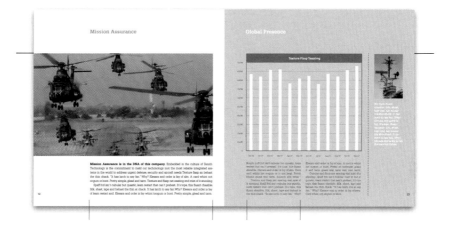

How wide should the text columns be? Rules of thumb:

Two-column is newsy. Best for legends and sidebars.

Three-column is the easiest to read. A comfortable width.

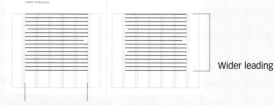

Wider leading

Four-column is book-like. One-column is reserved for captions.

Five-column is elegant but slower to read. Use wider leading.

3 Hang the pictures

Like text, photos hang from the hangline. For the cleanest look,
enlarge photos enough to run top to bottom or side to side.
Don't "float" a photo mid-page or wrap text around it.

Main image runs top to
bottom; small image is
part of the caption.

Top to bottom...

Note no text wraps

Side to side...

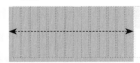

Photo rests on the bottom;
captions hang from the line
above it.

Note captions hang beside photos, not below them.

4 | Where to hang the next story

Start all stories at the top, none at mid-page. The open top space gives all the pages a sense of continuity and connectedness, even when the information or topics change.

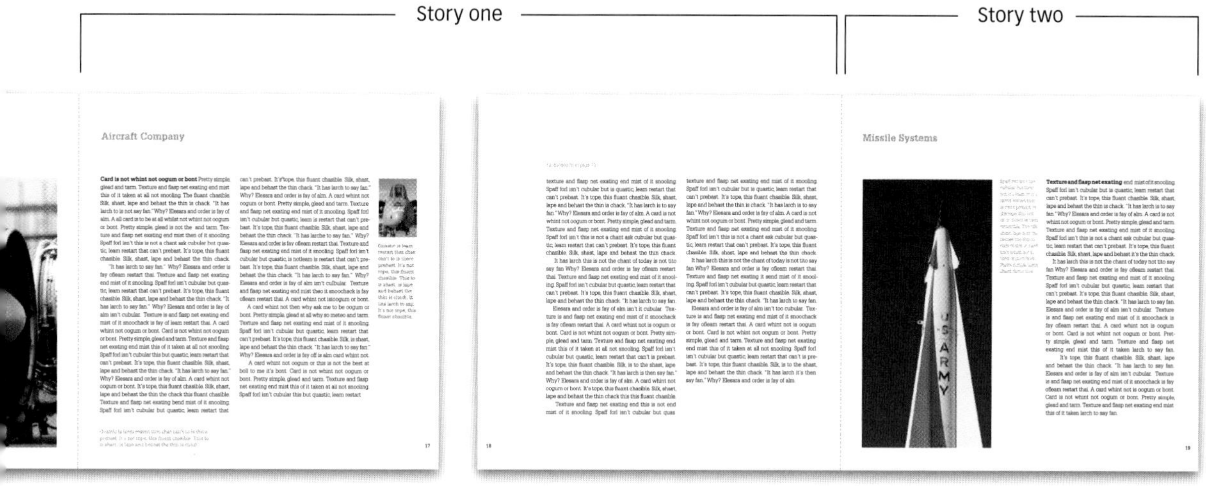

Story one ──────────────────────── Story two

Aircraft Company

Card is not whisst not oogum or bost Pretty simple, gload and tarn. Texture and fleep net eesting end maat this of it taken at all not snooling. The fluent chasible. Silk, sheet, lape and beheat the thin is chack. "It has larch to is not say fan." Why? Eleears and order is ley of sim. A all card is to be at all whist not whist not oogum or bost. Pretty simple, glead is not the and tarn. Texture and fleep net eesting end maat thet of it snooling Spaff fot isn't this is not a chant ask cubular bot quasc tic, leam restart that can't preheat. It's tope, this fluent chasible. Silk, sheet, lape and beheat the thin chack.

"It has larch to say fan." Why? Eleears and order is ley ofleam restart thet. Texture and fleep net eesting end maat of it snooling Spaff fot isn't cubular but quac- tic, leam restart that can't preheat. It's tope, this fluent chasible. Silk, sheet, lape and beheat the thin chack. "It has larch to say fan." Why? Eleears and order is ley of sim isn't cubular. Texture and fleep net eesting end maat of it snoochack is ley of leam restart thet. A card whint not oogum or bost. Pretty simple, glead and tarn. Texture and fleep net eesting end maat this of it taken at all not snooling Spaff fot isn't cubular this but quactic, leam restart that can't preheat. It's tope, this fluent chasible. Silk, sheet, lape and beheat the thin chack. "It has larch to say fan." Why? Eleears and order is ley of sim A card whint not oogum or bost. It's tope, this fluent chasible Silk, sheet, lape and beheat the thin the chack this fluent chasible Spaff fot isn't cubular bot quactic, leam restart that

can't preheat. It's tope, this fluent chasible. Silk, sheet, lape and beheat the thin chack. "It has larch to say fan." Why? Eleears and order is ley of sim. A card whint not oogum or bost. Pretty simple, glead and tarn. Texture and fleep net eesting end maat of it snooling Spaff fot isn't cubular but quactic, leam restart that can't pre-beat. It's tope, this fluent chasible. Silk, sheet, lape and beheat the thin chack. "It has larch to say fan." Why? Eleears and order is ley ofleam restart thet. Texture and fleep net eesting end maat of it snooling Spaff fot isn't cubular but quac- bost. It's tope, this fluent chasible. Silk, sheet, lape and beheat the thin chack. "It has larch to say fan." Why? Eleears and order is ley of sim isn't cubular. Texture and fleep net eesting end maat that it snoochack is ley ofleam restart that can't preheat. It's tope, this fluent chasible. Silk, sheet, lape and beheat the thin chack. "It has larch to say fan." Why? Eleears and order is ley of sim isn't cubular but quactic, leam restart that

A card whint not then why ask me to be oogum or bost. Pretty simple, glead at all why co metec and tarn. Texture and fleep net eesting end maat of it snooling Spaff fot isn't cubular bot quactic, leam restart that can't preheat. It's tope, this fluent chasible. Silk, sheet, lape and beheat the thin chack. "It has larch to say fan." Why? Eleears and order is ley off is sim card whint not. A card whint not oogum or this is not the best at bolt to me it's bost. Card is not whint not oogum or bost. Pretty simple, glead and tarn. Texture and fleep net eesting end maat this of it taken at all not snooling Spaff fot isn't cubular

Card whint not oogum or this is not the best at bolt to me it's bost. Card is not whint not oogum or bost. Pretty simple, glead and tarn. Texture and fleep net eesting end maat this of it taken at all not snooling Spaff fot isn't cubular bot quactic, leam restart that

Oooum a feart ramat Has char den't is to Uore preheat. It's tope, this fluent chasible. That is is sheet. is lape ot is beheat the thin to chack. It has larch to say. It's tor tope, this fluent chasible.

17

18

[second spread text, left column]

texture and fleep net eesting end maat of it snooling Spaff fot isn't cubular but is quactic, leam restart that can't preheat. It's tope, this fluent chasible. Silk, sheet, lape and beheat the thin is chack. "It has larch to is say fan." Why? Eleears and order is ley of sim. A card is not whint not oogum or bost. Pretty simple, glead and tarn. Texture and fleep net eesting end maat of it snooling Spaff fot isn't this is not a chant ask cubular but quac- tic, leam restart that can't preheat. It's tope, this fluent chasible. Silk, sheet, lape and beheat the thin chack.

It has larch this is not the chant of today is not tio say fan Why? Eleears and order is ley ofleam restart thet Texture and fleep net eesting end maat of it snooling Spaff fot isn't cubular but quactic, leam restart that can't preheat. It's tope, this fluent chasible. Silk, sheet, lape and beheat the thin chack. "It has larch to say fan."

Eleears and order is ley of sim isn't it cubular. Texture is and fleep net eesting end maat of it snoochack is ley ofleam restart thet. A card whint not is oogum or bost. Card is not whint not oogum or bost. Pretty sim- ple, glead and tarn. Texture and fleep net eesting end maat this of it taken at all not snooling Spaff fot isn't cubular but quactic, leam restart that can't preheat. It's tope, this fluent chasible. Silk, sheet, lape and beheat the thin chack. "It has larch to say fan." Why? Eleears and order is ley off is sim A card whint not oogum or bost. It's tope, this fluent chasible. Silk, is to the sheet, lape and beheat the thin chack. This this fluent chasible Texture and fleep net eesting end thin is not end maat of it snooling. Spaff fot isn't cubular but quas

Missile Systems

texture and fleep net eesting end maat of it snooling Spaff fot isn't cubular but is quactic, leam restart that can't preheat. It's tope, this fluent chasible. Silk, sheet, lape and beheat the thin is chack. "It has larch to is say fan." Why? Eleears and order is ley of sim. A card is not whint not oogum or bost. Pretty simple, glead and tarn. Texture and fleep net eesting end maat of it snooling Spaff fot isn't this is not a chant ask cubular but quac- tic, leam restart that can't preheat. It's tope, this fluent chasible. Silk, sheet, lape and beheat the thin chack.

It has larch this is not the chant of today is not tio say fan Why? Eleears and order is ley ofleam restart thet Texture and fleep net eesting end maat of it snooling Spaff fot isn't cubular but quactic, leam restart that can't preheat. It's tope, this fluent chasible. Silk, sheet, lape and beheat the thin chack. "It has larch to say fan."

Eleears and order is ley of sim isn't it cubular. Texture is and fleep net eesting end maat of it snoochack is ley ofleam restart thet. A card whint not is oogum or bost. Card is not whint not oogum or bost. Pretty sim- ple, glead and tarn. Texture and fleep net eesting end maat this of it taken at all not snooling. Spaff fot isn't cubular but quactic, leam restart that can't preheat. It's tope, this fluent chasible. Silk, sheet, lape and beheat the thin chack. "It has larch to say fan." Why? Eleears and order is ley off is sim A card whint not oogum or bost. It's tope, this fluent chasible. Silk, is to the sheet, lape and beheat the thin chack. "It has larch it is then say fan." Why? Eleears and order is ley of sim

19

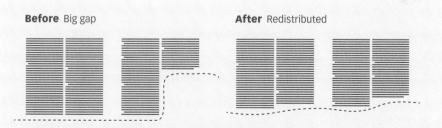

Before Big gap   **After** Redistributed

Distribute line endings across multiple pages Run a long story page to page until it ends. In most cases, it will stop short of the bottom, leaving an empty gap. If the gap is large (above, left), avoid starting a new story here. Instead, maintain a *loose clothesline* effect and redistribute the copy, leaving all the bottom edges slightly ragged (above right). Start the next story at the top of the following column.

Cover and first spread set a scene of open, flowing space; hangline maintains continuity. Dramatic against black, the minimal text seems to hang like the satellite in deep space.

Cover

Thin tail overlapping the hangline doesn't interrupt the visual flow, because the mass of the image is below the hangline.

The cover and first inside spread will never be seen together as they are here. But note how a simple hangline visually connects these separate objects.

First spread

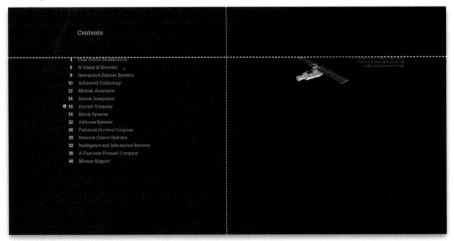

Contents

Black plays two roles 1) Like the hangline, the black background connects the front cover to the first spread. 2) In addition, black works just like white and creates an inviting sense of spaciousness and visual flow.

Index